MW00984667

THE BELIEF OF CATHOLICS

RONALD KNOX

THE BELIEF
OF
CATHOLICS

IGNATIUS PRESS   SAN FRANCISCO

Cover art: *Pentecost*
Psalter of Ingebourg of Denmark
Musée Conde, Chantilly, France
Giraudon / Art Resource, New York

Cover design by Roxanne Mei Lum

Published by Ignatius Press, San Francisco, 2000
ISBN 0-89870-586-x
Library of Congress control number 96-83634
Printed in the United States of America ∞

CONTENTS

FOREWORD TO THE
PRESENT EDITION

Of the British convert-writers who flourished in the first half of the twentieth century, few have been more influential than Ronald Knox (1888–1957). The son of the Anglican bishop of Manchester, he was called the cleverest boy ever to pass through Eton, and he excelled at Oxford, where he became known for his wit and classical scholarship—as early as his teenage years he was writing fine Latin and Greek verse. He was elected president of the Oxford Union and the debating society, and countless satirical verses and limericks were ascribed to him.

Knox' religious views matured early on. By the time he was sixteen he had subscribed to the Anglo-Catholic position, a considerable contrast from his father's Low Church position, and before his 1917 conversion to Catholicism he composed two brilliant works to support his views, *Absolute and Abitofhell* (1913), a satire modeled on Dryden's poem, and *Reunion All Around*, a look at ill-conceived attempts at religious unity, which even today sheds light on certain excesses of the ecumenical movement.

In 1918 appeared the story of Knox' conversion, *A Spiritual Aeneid*. A year later he was ordained a Catholic priest. For the next eight years he taught at St. Edmund's College in Ware and then was appointed chaplain to the undergraduates at his beloved Oxford, a post he held until 1939. While there he issued a seemingly endless stream of books, including collections of sermons, retreats, and even detective stories. (In his biography of Knox, Evelyn Waugh tweakingly noted that the detective stories, written in a logical style popular in the nineteen-twenties, had little appeal for women.)

Of special note is Knox' apologetical correspondence with Arnold Lunn, *Difficulties* (1932). He and Lunn were exact contemporaries, though Knox was a year ahead of Lunn at Oxford. Each in turn was the editor of the undergraduate journal *The Isis*. As Knox moved ever more toward Catholicism, Lunn moved toward a studied agnosticism. In their early forties they agreed to an exchange of letters in which Lunn presented his objections to the faith and Knox answered him. There was no effort by Knox to browbeat Lunn into submission. In fact, Lunn later attested that it was Knox' reserve that won him over. Winsome arguments in the end proved winning, and Lunn went on to become not only a convert but a noted Catholic apologist in his own right.

At the end of his Oxford chaplaincy, Knox wrote what is in artistry the best of his books, *Let Dons Delight*. Little read today, it is a series of conversations held in an imaginary Oxford common room at fifty-year intervals from the time of Elizabeth I to 1938. Especially remarkable is the manner in which Knox, through the conversation of his characters, conveyed subtle changes in the English language. He was a master not only of the English of our time but of the English of the preceding five centuries. *Let Dons Delight* is a telling look at how the British slowly fell away from authentic Christianity and clear thinking on religion once they severed their connection to Rome.

When Knox resigned the chaplaincy, it was with the intention of devoting himself to a fresh translation of the Bible. Brought up with the literary excellence of the Authorized Version and recognizing the deficiencies of the Douay-Rheims translation, he thought a new translation, in what he termed "timeless English", was needed if modern Catholics were to turn to the Bible in numbers. Obtaining the encouragement of the bishops of England and Wales, Knox moved to Aldenham in Shropshire, only to discover himself chaplain again, this time to girls whose school had been moved there at the outbreak of the war. Some of his best-received books— *The Creed in Slow Motion*, *The Mass in Slow Motion*, and *The Gospel in Slow Motion*—came from lectures delivered to them. His new duties delayed his work on the Bible, which was not completed until 1949. Many consider his version, which was a translation from the Vulgate, to be still the best available for devotional reading.

By his own reckoning, Knox's magnum opus was *Enthusiasm* (1950). He worked on it, off and on, for thirty years. He long had been interested in the phenomenon of religious enthusiasm, which is the claim of some people that they have a private revelation of God's will. Being above all a man of the Church, Knox was deeply convinced of her necessity and authority; he was suspicious of those claiming private revelations and found that they usually caused considerable harm. He hoped to demonstrate from history the chaos that results when one rejects the authority of Rome. "All my historical figures, Wesley himself included, were to be a kind of rogues' gallery, an awful warning against illuminism. But somehow, in the writing, my whole treatment of the subject became different; the more you got to know the men, the more human did they become, for better or worse; you were more concerned to find out why they thought as they did than to prove them wrong." Knox looked at movements both outside and inside the Church—from Methodism to Quietism, from Quakerism to Jansenism—and his analysis is especially useful today, when enthusiastic movements within Christianity are more widespread than ever.

His last apologetic work is his least known because it never was completed. *Proving God:A New Apologetic* was brought out posthumously in 1959, first in *The Month* and then as a long booklet. Waugh described it as "a work of systematic apologetics written in the language of the modern mind". This is not to say that the unfinished work represented Knox' first attempt to convey the faith colloquially. Each of his earlier apologetical writings was composed with this goal in mind. But by the end of his life he had come to see that things had altered so rapidly that each generation required its own approach. *Proving God* presents the same material in two forms— Knox was undecided about which to use—in straight prose and in the guise of a conversation. Knox was acutely conscious of the need for a well-rounded apologetic and was trying to find the right format for the middle of the century. He argued that mere argument was not enough. "Beat the atheist in argument, force him by sheer reason to admit the existence of a Deity, without at the same time convincing him of his need for redemption, and you have done him an injury. You have robbed him of his last poor thread of excuse—that he sinned in ignorance." Argument may be effective in breaking down excuses non-Catholics provide themselves, but it must go beyond that and lead to answers to life's deepest yearnings—and fears. Had it been completed, *Proving God* might have ended up as Knox' premier piece of apologetics. That honor must go, instead, to a much earlier work, *The Belief of Catholics* (1927), perhaps his best-known book.

While it deals extensively with Protestantism (one chapter is titled, plainspokenly, "Where Protestantism Goes Wrong"), its target is more the unchurched or lightly-churched modern who, if he gives any thought at all to Catholicism, thinks it mildly foreign. Knox begins traditionally, with a discussion of "the God who hides himself", and it is only halfway through that the divinity of Christ is established. As Knox knew, it is not the most difficult part of modern apologetics to convince the devoted Protestant that he has much of Christian truth but now needs to move on to the rest, which is found only in the Catholic Church. The most difficult part is convincing the nominal Protestant (or nominal Catholic, for that matter) or the vaguely religious person or the person without any religious inclinations that God really does exist, that his existence matters, and that only knowledge of him and obedience to him can lead to answers to the questions that haunt everyone.

Toward the end of the book, Knox discusses "the truths Catholics hold", "the rules Catholics acknowledge", "the strength Catholics receive", and "the ambitions Catholics honour". These truths, rules, strengths, and ambitions were attractive to the book's first readers. They were answers to the ever-present "Why?" These answers will prove equally attractive to today's readers who, after so many decades of failed *isms*, yearn for understanding and commitment even more than did their grandparents' generation. Whether or not Knox achieved a "timeless English" in his scriptural translation, in *The Belief of Catholics* he came close to a "timeless apologetic" for the faith.

KARL KEATING

FOREWORD TO THE
FIFTH EDITION

The Catholic Church and English letters both lost a many-sided genius when Ronald Knox died in 1957. His epitaph might well have been, as someone suggested: "R.I.P. Ronald Knox, translator of the Holy Bible and author of *The Viaduct Murder*."

Son of an Anglican bishop, Ronald Knox gave evidence of an ecclesiastical and literary bent almost from the cradle. At an age when most children are just learning to read, Knox was composing Greek and Latin epigrams. One triumph followed another at Eton and at Oxford. As a matter of course Oxonians came to credit him with every anonymous witticism. In 1912 he was ordained a clergyman in the Church of England. With his immense gifts and impeccable clerical background it was considered inevitable that he would one day be Archbishop of Canterbury.

It was not to be. He entered the Catholic Church in 1917 and received Holy Orders two years later. After a spell of teaching at the Westminster diocesan seminary he returned to a singularly fruitful thirteen years as chaplain to the Catholic students at Oxford. The English hierarchy then commissioned the great work of his life, the new translation of the Bible. He retired in 1939 to the Shropshire home of Lord Acton, to emerge nine years later after having produced what is widely regarded as the most elegant modern rendering of Holy Scripture.

Thus the statistics. What were the qualities that moved the London *Times* to call him "one of the outstanding figures of his generation"? His erudition—the Bible was but one facet of it—was immense and profound, the more attractive and impressive because carried so lightly. His wit—legendary even in his youth—was born of a mind that was probing, subtle, and razor-sharp. He was among the foremost literary stylists of our century; no less an authority than Evelyn Waugh has said that he considers him and Max Beerbohm the two finest modern writers of English.

And his versatility was awesome. He published some dozen collections of sermons, the most famous of which, *The Mass in Slow Motion*, reveals his knack of delivering the kind of talk that could captivate schoolgirls and at the same time win the plaudits of bishops and theologians. As a kind of adjunct to his Bible translation he wrote several commentaries. He was also the author of seven murder mysteries, many works of controversy, and perhaps the most intellectual of all modern accounts of conversion, *A Spiritual Aeneid*.

His satires are a special delight. *Barchester Pilgrimage* out-Trollopes Trollope, demonstrating the Knoxian flair for capturing the most delicate nuances in the styles of other writers—a gift he was later to put to more significant use in translating the Bible. *Essays in Satire* has fun with many of the more pretentious humbugs of modern religion, scholarship, and literature. *Memories of the Future* ("being memoirs of the years 1915–72, written in the year 1988 by Opal, Lady Porstock") is a hilarious travesty on social, intellectual, and religious folly. *Let Dons Delight* is a highly amusing, literarily breath-taking *tour de force* among professors in an Oxford common room at fifty-year intervals from 1588 to 1938. The characterizations are superb, each reflecting currents of thought and even developments in the language, and all done with unfailing wit. It is a remarkable book, one which only Knox could have written.

His own favorite, *Enthusiasm*, has been hailed by Evelyn Waugh as the great literary masterpiece of our century. It is the history of a recurrent religious aberration, the strong sense of direct divine guidance that has bemused many an ardent Christian through the centuries. The subject, such a rich mine of eccentricity, must have appealed hugely to Knox' fine sense of the ridiculous; yet his balance and sympathetic insight add a dimension of depth to a theme that in this book receives its first mature treatment.

The present volume, a masterly exposition of Catholic doctrine, is being reprinted here for the fifth time—an eloquent tribute to its enduring value. The theme is timeless yet urgent, and it has never in our day been presented so brilliantly.

PREFACE

It may easily be felt that a Catholic apologist does best to put himself on the defensive, in days so unfriendly as these towards the general outlook of Catholicism. Thus, there are philosophers who question the adequacy of thought itself as a method of arriving at speculative truth; there are psychologists who deny the reality of human free will; there are anthropologists who would explain away religion as an illusion of the nursery; and meanwhile, aiming their shafts more directly at the Church to which I belong, historians are for ever turning up flaws in our title-deeds, and prophets of the age arraign our narrow outlook before the tribunal of human progress. To meet any one of these assaults upon its own ground would need a book at least as long as this. I have not the qualifications, if I had the whim, to pick up such gauntlets; journalism has docketed the world for us long since, and no author is allowed to try conclusions with a specialist unless he is fortified with a whole array of letters after his name in works of reference. This book, then, is an attempt to write constructive apologetic, to assert a claim; and if the specialist feels inclined, as doubtless he will, to buttonhole me here and there with the demand for fuller explanations, I must offer him the discourtesy of hurrying on; there is no space for them.

Neither, unfortunately, am I a theologian; and it follows that the theses here put forward, apart from the brevity which circumstances impose upon them, are put forward in crude language, without niceties of definition. But I have been asked to state "what I believe"; and, in so far as this series is intended to include human documents, my own contribution will be all the better, I take it, for the want of academic precision. Let my convictions be untidy in their arrangement, loose in their expression; at least they are genuine.

THE OLD PALACE, OXFORD
July 1927

PREFACE TO THE NEW EDITION

So many Protestant controversialists have seen fit to misrepresent me by printing extracts from pages 203 and 204 of the earlier edition, torn from their context with an array of dots and falsifying the general sense of the passage, that I have decided to alter two sentences; not by way of withdrawing anything I have said, but by way of making it clear beyond the possibility of mistake. Or is this hoping for too much? In any case, apologists who are confronted with what I wrote in 1927 will do well to insist that the objector shall do me the justice to quote from the new edition.

I

The Modern Distaste for Religion

In a too crowded age—I refer, not to the multiplication of mortal lives, but to the multiplicity of human interests—it is an uneasy business to estimate tendencies or to prophesy developments. So many agitators, publicists, and quack physicians, each with his own platform and his own audience, din into our ears the importance of a thousand rival or unconnected movements, so ruled by chance is the sub-editor's preference for this or that head-line, the loyalty of the public towards the catchwords it favoured yesterday, that a wise man might well ask to be excused the task of pronouncing upon the chaos, or of guessing the outcome. Last century, for instance, one thing seemed luminously clear, that Liberalism was advancing, and was bound to advance, in a constant ratio of progress. Does Europe, does England, ratify that opinion now? And if there has been a reaction, is the defeat final or temporary? Which of the modern movements are genuine currents, which the backwash of a flood? Which of our modern evils are symptoms, and which are organic diseases? Which of our modern results are the true offspring of an age, which are sports and freaks of history? Historians of to-morrow, excuse our frantic guess-work in your clearer vision.

Amidst the tangle, one strand seems to define itself—within the last hundred years, within the last fifty years, within the last twenty-five years, the force of religion, as a factor in English public life, has steadily and visibly declined. I do not mean that a careless and external diagnosis would detect the change. Within the last few years we have seen, perhaps, a greater output of religious discussion in public print than any age since the Reformation. But this itch for religious discussion, which is peculiarly British, is not really an encouraging symptom. Men do not talk about their health when their health is strongest; a nation does not talk about its religion when its religion is flourishing. Statistics, it is true, may be misleading, but they are the thermometer of change. And any statistical comparison I have ever undertaken, or seen undertaken, seems to yield the same result—namely, that the area of lives visibly affected by habits of religion shrinks from decade to decade, and almost from year to year. To take an instance at random—Trollope, in his "Vicar of Bullhampton" (published in 1870), writes of a London population "not a fourth of whom attend divine service". Is it not the impression most of us would record, after a Sunday morning spent in the metropolis, that today we should have to write "a tenth" instead of "a fourth"?

I was told the other day of a more exact calculation, made in a more particular field, but not, to my mind, less significant. A statistician went through the records of the old boys from one of our greatest public schools, jotting down the number of those who adopted Holy Orders as their vocation in life. His observations began with 1860, and finished, necessarily, in the first decade of the present century. He marked off the period into spaces of five years, and found that in each five years the number of those who were ordained was perceptibly smaller than in the period immediately preceding it. In the first of the periods the ratio of clerical vocations was sixteen per cent; in the last, it was something over three per cent. In short, within a space of forty-five years the ideal of the Christian ministry had lost four-fifths of its popularity.

It will be said, only among the expensively educated classes. True, the old sources of supply were not the only sources of supply, and it may be all the better for a Church to have a ministry recruited from the people. But the facts in themselves are surely suggestive. It is difficult not to suppose that there has been some change in the atmosphere of England—a change, perhaps, more easily and more acutely felt in the admirably ventilated dormitories of our public schools than elsewhere. It would be absurd to suppose that the falling-off in clerical vocations is the result of mere accident; uncharitable to suppose that it corresponded to a decrease in the value of clerical incomes, in the prestige of the clerical state. You must consider that the old public schools hand on a tradition of English citizenship, of which English Churchmanship is an integral part; that the appeal of the recruiting sergeant is seldom long absent from their chapel sermons; that clerical heroes are constantly held up to the admiration of these youthful audiences, and clerical ambitions extolled. If, in spite of all this, that clergy which was once the *stupor mundi* now finds it hard to fill up the gaps in its files, can we doubt that there has been a modification in the public attitude towards religion?

Nor is the shortage of clergy unaccompanied by a shortage of laity. A mere glance at the official figures issued by the various religious bodies reveals the nakedness of our church pews. The Church of England, judging from its baptismal register, still numbers some twenty-five million nominal members; but its Easter Communions are less than a tenth of this total. Even when we make allowance for children who are not yet of communicant age, it is difficult to suppose that the effective membership of the Anglican Church constitutes one-tenth of the English population. Neither the Church of England nor any Nonconformist body registers any increase of membership which keeps pace with the annual birth-rate; some of them have to register a net loss, not only of ministers, but of chapels and of Sunday scholars. What hopes can be conceived that religion continues to be a real force in a nation which has so feeble a grasp on Church membership as this?

I know it is said that Church membership is one thing, and religion another. Optimists will almost be prepared to claim that it is a healthy sign, this breaking away from the tests and shibboleths of the past; men are more reluctant, they explain, to give in their names to this -*ism* or that, precisely in proportion as their own religious lives are firmly rooted and plentifully nourished. All that is excellently said; and few will dispute that it is possible to be a Theist, and indeed a Christian in the broader, modern sense of the word, without subscribing to a creed or offering your prayers in a church. But can any sensible person delude himself into the idea that a decline of organised religion does not mean, *pro tanto*, a decline of religion altogether? For twenty people who will tell you that they can get all the religion they want without going to the parsons for it, is there one who ever offers a prayer, or consciously makes an act of love to Almighty God? There is a mystical temperament which finds itself best in isolation, but it is a rare and a delicate growth. The ordinary man, being a social animal, is social also in his religious instincts. If he is in earnest about the business of his own spiritual life, he instinctively crowds up against his fellows for warmth, worships in the same building with them, and writes down his name on a common subscription list. He does this the more readily in a country where he has so wide a variety of denominations amongst which he can choose, some of them applying the least exacting of tests even to communicant membership. If we were really growing more religious, should not at least the gleanings of that harvest tell upon the statistics of organised religion? In default of the gleanings, who will convince us of the harvest?

The main causes of this decline, so far as causes need to be adduced for the defection of human wills, are manifest enough. Undoubtedly popular education and the spread of newspaper culture must be credited, in part, with the result: some of us would say that the mass of the people is now growing out of its old superstitions in the light of new knowledge; some of us would see, rather, the effect of reiterated catchwords upon minds trained to read but not trained to think. The industrial development of the country has added its influence, partly by focusing men's thoughts upon their material interests, partly by setting up, in England as elsewhere, a reaction against old faiths and old loyalties, crudely conceived as old-fashioned. Further, the modern facilities for pleasurable enjoyment have killed, in great part, the relish for eternity. I do not know that this influence has been given its proper importance hitherto. Mass production has made luxury cheap; steam travel, motor-cars, and the penny post have brought it to our doors; anæsthetics and the other triumphs of medicine have mitigated the penalties which attach to it. And the same causes which have multiplied pleasure have multiplied preoccupation. A rush age cannot be a reflective age.

So much for the pew; meanwhile, what has been happening in the pulpit?

It would not be true, I think, to say that dogma is less preached today than it was a hundred years ago. The rise of Wesleyanism and the Evangelical Movement had, indeed, put an end by then to the long indifference of the latitudinarian age. But Wesleyanism and Evangelicism were interested only in a handful of dogmas which concerned their own particular scheme of salvation. On the other hand, men did believe in the Bible, not as "given of God to convey to us in many parts and in divers manners the revelation of himself", but as inspired in an intelligible sense. And with the rise of the Oxford Movement this belief in Scripture was fortified by a confident appeal, unsound in its method but sincere in its purpose, to the deposit of Christian tradition. But during the last fifty years and more, the fundamental dogmas of the Christian religion have been subjected, more and more, to criticism, or interpretation, and to restatement. Would a diocesan Bishop have dared in the middle of the nineteenth century, to express in a newspaper article his disbelief in eternal punishment? Would the rector of a much-frequented London church have preached, and afterwards published, a sermon in which he recommended the remarriage of divorced persons? Would the whole Bench of Bishops have been prepared to alter, in the Baptismal Service, the statement that every child is conceived and born in sin? Appraise the tendency as you will; welcome or regret its influence; but only disingenuity can deny that the tendency is there, and is apparently constant. You do not believe what your grandfathers believed, and have no reason to hope that your grandsons will believe what you do.

In the early days of the Tractarian Movement it looked, for a time, as if this decline of dogma might be arrested by force; as if the invading germ of modernism might be expelled from within. Even seventy years back, or little more, in the days of Pusey, Burgon, Mansell, Denison, and Liddon, there was a vigorous outcry whenever countenance was shown to the first whispers of infidelity. Not so long ago, a collection of essays appeared, written by representative High Churchmen, so unguarded in certain points, particularly in its attitude towards Scripture, that any one of the five champions I have just mentioned would certainly have clamoured for its condemnation. It seems as if the modern High Church party were content to insist on the adoption of ceremonies and devotions such as are found in Catholic countries, and no longer concerned themselves with safeguarding, if they can still be safeguarded, the doctrines of Catholic antiquity. Nor do they merely tolerate in others the expression of views which their fathers would have branded as unorthodox; they themselves, more and more, are becoming infected by the contagion of their surroundings, and lose the substance of theology while they embrace its shadow. And still, by a pathetic error, they cherish the dream of reunion, when it must be clear to any prudent mind that the gulf between Rome and Canterbury never stood so wide as it stands today.

The ministers of the Free Churches will hardly, I suppose, be concerned to deny that in this matter they are abreast, if not ahead, of their Anglican rivals. Less retarded by the trammels of antiquity, less apprehensive of schism, more accustomed to recognise in religious innovation the influence of the Holy Spirit, they are free to catch the wind of the moment and sink their nets where the fishing seems best. The very titles of their discourses, as you see them pasted up Sunday after Sunday on the chapel notice-boards—high-flown, literary titles, such as tickle the ear of the passers-by—contrast strangely with the old, stern message of Baxter and Wesley—sin, hell, love, grace, faith, and conversion. I have myself seen such a chapel bill which promised first a comfortable seat, then good music, then a hearty welcome, and last of all, as if it were an afterthought, a "Gospel message". It is hardly to be expected that those who approached their prospective audience in so accommodating a spirit should expound much of dogma in their pulpits—dogma, so much vilified in the newspapers, so little palatable to the man in the street.

It appears, then, that the two processes are going on side by side, the decline of Church membership and the decline of dogma; the evacuation of the pew and the jettisoning of cargo from the pulpit. I have been at pains to adduce instances of the fact, though indeed it was hardly necessary, for the two tendencies are pretty generally admitted; the one openly deplored, the other openly defended. Are the two processes interrelated? And, if so, does the decline of Church membership cause the decline of dogma, or result from it, or is it a parallel symptom? Reflection shows, I think, that there is truth in all three suggestions.

To some extent, the decline of Church membership causes the decline of dogma. Obviously, the grievance of the man in the street against organised religion is partly an intellectual one. Other influences may prevail to keep him away from Church; as, a general unreasoning dislike towards all forms of authority, or absorption in pleasures and in worldly distractions. But the reason he alleges, at any rate, for his nonattendance is commonly his inability to believe "the stuff the parsons preach". What wonder if this attitude makes the preacher reconsider his message? He would blame himself if he allowed souls to lose contact with religion through undue insistence on any doctrine that was not true—or even not certainly true—or even not theologically important. Hence comes the impetus to take stock afresh of his own theological position; is he really convinced of the truth, the certainty, the importance of such and such a doctrine? He is bound, indeed, to declare the whole counsel of God. But what is the whole counsel of God? If he could accept the inerrancy of

Scripture, like his fathers before him, he would have at least a chart to guide him. But he has no ground for believing in the inerrancy of Scripture, unless it be guaranteed to him by the Church. What Church? His Church? If the Church of England be meant, or a fortiori any of the Nonconformist bodies, he can find no help in such a refuge; for a religious connection which claims no infallibility for itself can hardly be justified in investing the Bible with inerrancy! If, on the contrary, he appeals to the Catholic Church, he knows that he is appealing to a tribunal by whose judgments he himself does not abide. Somehow, then, he has to construct his own theology for himself, and to take responsibility for the construction; in doing so, would he be human if he were not influenced a little by the unbelief of those about him, by those unfilled pews which reproach him, Sunday by Sunday, with preaching a message unacceptable to the spirit of the age?

I do not mean to suggest that the desire to meet infidelity half-way is the sole or even the main cause responsible for the loose theology of our time. No preacher would deliberately judge the credibility of his message by the credulity of his audience. But the prevalent irreligion of the age does exercise a continual unconscious pressure upon the pulpit; it makes preachers hesitate to affirm doctrines whose affirmation would be unpopular. And a doctrine which has ceased to be affirmed is doomed, like a disused organ, to atrophy.

That modernism among the clergy and scepticism among the laity are to some extent parallel effects of the same causes, hardly needs demonstration. The confident assertions of the philosopher, the scientist, the historian—that truth is relative, not absolute; that we can no longer believe in Genesis; that Christianity descends straight from the heathen mystery religions—will differ in their effect on different minds. One man will say, quite simply, "Then it's no good believing in Christianity any longer"; another will prefer to consider how the abiding truth of Christianity can best be reconciled with these apparently discouraging notions, how best restated in the light of these recent additions to human knowledge. Sometimes it is a matter of training and outlook; A is already looking out for, nay, is almost prepared to welcome, an excuse for abandoning his old religious ideas; B would sooner bid farewell to reason itself than impugn the veracity of the Church which has nourished him. Sometimes it is a matter of temperament; the world may be divided (amongst other convenient dichotomies) into the people who take it or leave it and the people who split the difference. Sometimes there is a real intellectual struggle in one conscientious mind as to whether any accommodation can consistently be made between the new truth and the old tradition.

It must not be supposed that we have finished with materialism. Yesterday, it was the concept of Evolution that was in the air. To one mind, it seemed a disproof of the very basis of religious truth; it had knocked the bottom out of Christianity. To another mind, this same concept of Evolution seemed a convenient solder for patching up the holes in a leaky system; apply its doctrines to the Christian faith, and it would begin to hold water once more. Today, the rage is for psychology; to some minds the new psychology has already destroyed, or is beginning to destroy, the whole notion of free will. Others, within the Christian camp, are beginning to take up the jargon of the new empiricism and apply it to the problems of religion, not less joyfully than their fathers did yesterday. What is one man's poison is another man's drug.

In a sense, then, the decline of Church membership explains the decline of dogma. In a sense, it is a parallel effect of the same causes. But there is a sense, also, in which the decline of dogma explains the decline of Church membership.

Such a suggestion is, of course, clean contrary to the fashionable platitudes of our day. When "the failure of the Churches" is discussed in public print, our well-meaning advisers always insist, with a somewhat wearying reiteration, on the need for a more comprehensive Christianity, which shall get away from forms and ceremonies, from dogmas and creeds, and shall concentrate its attention upon those elementary principles of life and devotion which all Christians have at heart. Each prophet who thus enlightens us makes the curious assumption, apparently, that he is the first person who has ever suggested anything of the kind. As a matter of fact, the brazen lungs of Fleet Street have been shouting these same directions at us for a quarter of a century past. And have "the Churches" taken no notice? On the contrary, as I have suggested above, the pilots of our storm-tossed denominations have lost no opportunity of lightening ship by jettisoning every point of doctrine that seemed questionable, and therefore unessential; hell has been abolished, and sin very nearly; the Old Testament is never alluded to but with a torrent of disclaimers, and miracle with an apologetic grimace. Preachers of the rival sects have exchanged pulpits; "joint services" have been held on occasions of public importance; even the inauguration of a new Anglican cathedral cannot take place nowadays without a fraternisation of the Christianities. In hundreds of churches and chapels everything has been done that could be done to meet this modern latitudinarian demand. And the result?

The result is that as long as a man is a good preacher, a good organiser, or an arresting personality, he can always achieve a certain local following; and among this local following a reputation for broad-mindedness stands him in good stead. But the ordinary man who does not go to church is quite un-affected by the process. He thinks no better of Christianity for its efforts to be undogmatic. It is not that he makes any articulate reply to these overtures; he simply ignores them. Nothing, I believe, has contributed more powerfully to the recent successes of the "Anglo-Catholic" movement than the conviction, gradually borne in upon the clergy, that the lati-tudinarian appeal, as a matter of experience, does not attract. Dogmas may fly out at the window but congregations do not come in at the door.

So much, as a matter of daily experience, will hardly be gainsaid. What follows is more controversial; indeed, it is a thesis which hardly admits of exact proof. It seems to me that (let us say) seven in ten of our fellow-countrymen, if they give a thought to the matter at all, think the worse, not the better, of our modern leaders for their willingness to throw dogma overboard to the wolves of unbelief. They are scandalised, rather than impressed, by the theological chaos which two generations of controversy have left behind them. It is the common assumption of all these modern prophets, whatever their school, that religious truth is something not yet determined, something which is being gradually estab-lished by a slow process of testing and research. They boast of their indecisions; they parade their dissensions; it shows (they say) a healthy spirit of fearless inquiry, this freedom from the incubus of tradition. Such sentiments evoke, I believe, no echo of applause outside their own immediate circles. The uneasy impression is left on the average citizen that "the parsons do not know their own business"; that disagreements between sect and sect are more, not less disedifying when either side hastens to explain that the disagreement is over externals, rather than essentials; that if Christianity is still in process of formulation after twenty centuries, it must be an uncommonly elusive affair. The average citizen expects any religion which makes claims upon him to be a revealed religion; and if the doctrine of Christianity is a revealed doctrine, why all this perennial need of discussion and restatement? Why should a divine structure send in continual bills for alterations and repairs? Moreover, he is a little suspicious of these modern concessions, these attempts to meet him halfway. Is the stock (he asks in his commercial way) really a sound investment, when those who hold it are so anxious to unload it on any terms?

It is not only the theological speculations of the modern Christianities which produce this sense of uneasiness. It is the whole accommodating attitude taken up by the religions of today and their professors—accommodating, and for that reason, not reassuring. It is an infinitely small point, but does the abandonment, total or partial, of the clerical garb by some modern clergymen really make the laity feel more at home with them? Does it not rather create the suspicion that they are ashamed of being what they are? Distrust may even be aroused, sometimes, by the modern sympathy of official Anglicanism for the movement towards democracy; to some minds, it comes too late to be impressive. The gesture made by "the Churches" at the time of the General Strike was, I fully believe, the result of a sincere desire for the national well-being. But this confidence was not everywhere felt; many preferred to think it dictated by panic, rather than by genuine concern. Even in matters of grave and practical moral import, representatives of the Christian bodies have, before now, given forth an uncertain sound, and affirmed the traditional ethics of Christianity with a minority protest. Most outside critics sympathised, no doubt, with the minority; but it is questionable whether they felt much respect for a religion whose spokesmen could differ so fundamentally.

Do the Churches know their own mind, or even their own minds? That is, in effect, the question which bewilders men today far more than any strictly theological problem. I do not mean that the ordinary Englishman is for ever worrying about the question; the sad truth is that he lacks the necessary interest in religious matters altogether. You will only catch occasional glimpses of his attitude; but they are, to my mind, unmistakable. "Let the Churches make up their own mind what they believe", he says, "and then come and tell me." Meanwhile, there is no sign that such an event is probable. The present effort to unify belief and practice within the Church of England is the heir to a long line of failures. The Anglo–Catholic party has a solidarity that is only external; it is based on a compromise, and its unity is that of a party, not that of a creed. This generation will die, and the next, before "the Churches" can present the nation with a common programme.

We have no precedent by which to forecast the outcome of the present situation. The pulse of religion has beaten low enough in England before now, but there has never, before this last century, been a time at which so many of our fellow-countrymen made no response to its movements. In the worst of the latitudinarian days the embers of belief were kept alive, not smothered, by the ashes of indifference. The Bible was never so little believed as it is today; I doubt if it was ever so little read. The optimism of the religious temperament will continually find new grounds for confidence; will hail local successes, and welcome the suggestion of untried remedies; but there is no sign, yet, of a rally, no distant foot-fall of the Prodigal's return. Organised religion has shrunk, and is still shrinking, at once in the content of its message and in the area of its appeal.

II

The Shop Window

It so happens that there is one religious body in the country which registers a yearly increase in its membership more than proportionate to the national birth-rate. It so happens that there is one religious body in the country which does not alter its message to suit the shifting fashions of human thought, which gives no sign of yielding to modern outcries under the severest pressure from public opinion. It so happens that the body alluded to is in either case the same, the Catholic Church.

I am not instituting a precarious inference from the popularity of my own religion to its truth. No inference is more easy, none is, commonly, more fallacious. I am simply trying to account for the fact, which is an observable fact to any unprejudiced critic, that the Catholic Church has, at the moment, a readier hearing and a better all-round reception among the mass of Englishmen than it has had since its voice was smothered by persecution—it seemed, finally—two hundred and fifty years ago. In contrast with the general religious conditions which I have attempted to depict in the last chapter, men's attention is directed towards us, either because our pulpits still give forth the same sound, or because our pews are filling instead of emptying, or because a comparison of these two facts seems to them significant. I am not optimist enough to exaggerate the tendency. I fancy it is still true that the mass of the population thinks of us as something quite off the map; conceives our pomp of yesterday as one with Nineveh and Tyre. But, as Catholic churches spring into being all over the country, as Catholic activities demand a larger publicity even from that highly conventional institution, the daily press, we appear to provide the bewildered Englishman sometimes with a criticism, sometimes with a solution, of the religious problems which distract our times.

It is difficult to form any idea of the neglect, nay, of the contempt into which the Catholic name had fallen in England towards the end of the eighteenth century, before the French Revolution, the Oxford conversions, and the Irish immigration had strengthened our position. I do not mean politically; the 'Forty-five, and memories of the 'Forty-five, still made us formidable to our fellow-countrymen. But Catholicism as an intellectual system seemed, I suppose, no more possible to the Englishmen of the eighteenth century than the principles of the Thug or the Doukhobor. So far removed was it from the intellectual compass of the age, that those who professed it—in our country, a particularly hardheaded set of men—were assumed to be fanatics, drugged by the influence of some strange wave of religious emotion; it was not conceived possible that calm deliberation, that reasoned calculation, could lead a man to conclusions so unfashionable. In an age which hated enthusiasm, Catholicism was the *reductio ad absurdum* of enthusiasm; and there is pleasant reading to be found in the magazines of the period, where the early fervours of Wesleyanism are compared to those of "Popery", and condemned by the comparison. Two Wesleyan preachers, at Brighton, I think, were actually said to have been recognised by passers-by as members of the Society of Jesus. Faded Chloes and Clorindas, how you despised us!

In our day, antipathy to Catholicism is still abundantly manifested. Wills are drawn up in which the heir forfeits his rights if he should make his submission to Rome; and when a conversion does take place, at least in those highest and lowest social strata in which prejudice dies hard, it is usually the signal for a chorus of irascible comment. But, when the concrete case does not arise, it is wonderful how much Platonic admiration is shown nowadays for the Catholic system, once so contemned; it is wonderful how often the velleity (as the schoolmen say) to become a Catholic is found among highly educated and highly cultivated people, who never in fact come near to the point of submission. Allowance must be made for kind-heartedness and natural politeness; but this explanation cannot be accepted as the sole explanation; you hardly ever meet an intelligent person who does not admire us for *something*. He would so like to be a Catholic (he says) for the sake of points A, B, and C in our system, if only points D, E, and F did not interpose an insuperable barrier.

And, although such language is often on the lips of men who have never seriously considered whether submission to the Church is, or ever could be, possible for them, there are lives in which the nostalgia for Rome makes tragedy. Such a craving was Florence Nightingale's; such was W. H. Mallock's, though indeed he did have a priest at his deathbed. At this moment, without stopping to think of names, I can recall three men of good family and exceptional ability who have died, within the last decade or so, outside the Church, although their familiar friends knew that they were longing to become Catholics if they could. Such intellects, like moths singeing their wings round a candle, cannot keep away from the thought of Catholicism, however often it repels them. It

drives them away from every other form of religion, as hope-
less love for a married woman may keep a man a bachelor;
they will not put up with second-best substitutes. There is an
attraction about the Catholic Church, not merely for the
pigeon-headed *dévot* or the paradoxical undergraduate, but
for penetrating minds and justly balanced temperaments.

I propose in this chapter to disentangle some of the various
elements in the appeal of which I have been speaking. I have
called it the Shop Window, because I believe that there is, I
will not say a large body of people, but a considerable body of
people, whom you may easily liken to a crowd of small boys
outside a confectioner's shop, flattening their noses against the
pane and feasting, in imagination only, upon the good things
they see there—but they have no money to get in. Just so
these Platonic admirers, these would-be converts, look long-
ingly towards Catholicism for the satisfaction each of his own
need; now and again, perhaps (it notoriously happens in shop
windows) mistaking some accidental glory of the Church for
a more perfect thing than it is. The elders, in hearing Helen's
suit, must needs make allowance for the siren sweetness of her
voice. So he who undertakes to investigate the claims of the
Catholic Church is naturally on his guard lest his judgment
should be biased unconsciously in its favour. At least we shall
avoid unconscious bias if, from the outset, we tabulate the
various attractions which the Church has for various minds,
put them out (as it were) in the shop window, and take a good
look at them. They talk of the "lure" of Rome; in this
chapter, at any rate, the net shall be spread honestly in the
sight of the bird.

Of all the features in the Catholic system which appeal
powerfully to men's minds at the present moment, the least,
assuredly, is the mere beauty of her external adornment; the
merely æsthetic effect of vestments made in art stuffs, of

blazing candles, of gold and silver altar furniture, of lace and flowers. Chloe and Clorinda did feel, I think, a sneaking attraction towards these Romish bedizenments, tempered, of course, by a strong moral reprobation. In our day, their appeal is of the slightest. If for no other reason, because these characteristics of our own system are easily imitable and have been freely imitated. It is, perhaps fortunately, no longer necessary to betake yourself to Catholic churches in order to glut your senses with artistic appreciation of ceremonial. Our High Church friends do it as well or better; their churches provide, as it were, a mimic Riviera on the soil of home to suit these sickly temperaments. Mere beauty, mere pageantry, is no speciality of ours, and no appreciable boast.

But there is something else underlying the pomp of our ceremonial which makes, I think, a more powerful impression, though one far more difficult to analyse. I mean the sense of mystery. The effect of long distances, of tapers flickering in the heart of an altar far away, of slow silences interrupted by sudden bursts of sound, of voices coming from unseen quarters, of doors opening unexpectedly, of figures moving to and fro over a business unintelligible to the spectator, of long chants in a language which he does not hear, or does not understand, of tingling bells, and incense-smoke caught in the shifting lights of a high-windowed building— the effect, I say, of all this upon the visitor who has no opportunity and no wish to "follow the service" is to breed an atmosphere of solemn mystery which works, not upon his senses, but upon his imagination. In this respect, Catholic ceremonial does not lend itself so readily to imitation. The intrusion of English, or any other intelligible tongue, breaks the spell of mystery with its too familiar cadences. And yet you will meet with elements of all this in some of the old cathedrals; you will meet it in King's Chapel, at Cambridge, if you stand outside the screen and listen to the chanting on the farther side of it. Conversely, in a small and ill-built Catholic church you will miss the illusion.

Our crude forefathers had a name for all this; they called it hocus-pocus. The moderns, or at least the more religiously disposed among them, have formed a very different judgment. To them this illusion is "the sense of worship"; it proves, with reasons of the heart, not of the intellect, that man is born for something higher than materialism. This sense of unapproachableness, is it not evidence that there is an Unapproachable, whom yet our finite minds must needs labour to approach? I confess that I cannot find it in my heart to agree fully with either criticism. Mystification, mummery for mummery's sake, exasperates me beyond speech; and I have never been able to understand my countrymen's partiality for Masonic and quasi-Masonic ritual. But in Catholic churches the effect is an accidental one; we do not deliberately mystify; on the contrary, our modern tendency encourages the laity to know what is being done, and even, by the aid of translations, to follow what is being said. If anybody prefers to cultivate the sense of mystery, by all means let him. But it is a very tenuous argument that can be derived from the impressions so received, in favour either of Christianity or of Catholicism.

From a different angle, the outside observer is apt to conceive of Catholicism as being at least a *business-like* religion. The ministers of most Christian denominations affect, he finds, a slowness of walk and of movement while they are in church; they talk either in deliberately earnest tones, or in a kind of professional drawl; their enunciation, their gestures, even the look on their faces is expressive of unction. Nay, even out of church, he detects (or thinks he detects) a certain professionalism of manner, a "parsonified air", which repels him. It seems to him that he finds, among the other Christianities, a deliberate attempt to be impressive; and, Briton-like, he suspects unreality behind these calculated *démarches*. Good wine, he reminds himself, needs no bush; and if there were really any truth behind the doctrines which these teachers profess, they would not be so desperately anxious to parade their conviction of it. Whereas, if he has strayed into a Catholic church, he finds these airs of professionalism absent; there are no unnatural tones in the voice, there is no obtrusive deliberation of manner; the priest goes about his work with the briskness, the matter-of-factness, of a shopkeeper or an operating surgeon; the whole performance seems to be, for the initiated, something quite natural, something which they take for granted. And, though it may all mean to him no more than the liturgy of mumbo-jumbo, he is favourably impressed with the convictions of men and women who can thus hold commerce with the other world without inhuman deportment. "They seem to know what they are about, these people", is his criticism; and perhaps there is something in it.

So far I have been assuming that our inquirer has not been content to learn about the Church by hearsay, but has attended Catholic services, if only as part of his experiences during foreign travel. But indeed it is possible, without any first-hand contact, to find your imagination dwelling wistfully on the thought of the Catholic Church. Alone among the Christianities, it is capable of taking rank, even in isolation, as one of the great religions of the world. Take it vertically or horizontally, that is, historically or geographically, it is a vast edifice; like the Great Pyramid, it will challenge your attention from a distance, and set you wondering how human workmanship (as you suppose it to be) can spread so wide and so defy the centuries. Nor is it any megalomania, any spirit of religious jingoism, that makes us long to claim membership in such an institution. To belong to a small sect may have its attractions, may prove a sop to pride, or an incentive to fanaticism. But the normal man, less self-confident in his opinions, asks for company; he would not, if possible, have the whole world disagreeing with him. He will at least envisage the possibility that the majority may be right, though it be beyond the seas, or even beyond the grave.

Let us look at the historical character of Catholicism first. It is convenient, no doubt, to call oneself a Christian, and even (by a modern metaphor) to call oneself "a Catholic", without feeling responsible for the whole chequered past of Christendom; without making oneself an accessory to the fires of Smithfield, or being tarred with the brush of Torquemada. Happy is the nation (it has been said) which has no past; and a Church of yesterday enjoys the advantages which that dictum implies. To be tied to no dead hand of tradition, bowed down by no cumbrous legacies of antiquity, leaves the mind more free for speculation, and the heart for adventure. But in disclaiming the dead, you are yourself disclaimed by the dead. If you are not prepared to blush for Alexander the Sixth, it is childishly inconsistent to take pride in the memory of Saint Francis. You may claim a kind of sentimental connection with the Christianity of earlier ages, but not a historic, not a vital continuity. The Fathers of the early Church may be your models and your heroes, but they are no genuine part of your ancestry.

It is not everybody who has a sense of history—I mean, a feeling for our past. Indeed, there is a kind of modem coxcombry which takes delight in belittling the achievements of the human genius by comparing them with the long, vacant centuries which preceded history itself. But it is hard to see how those who are accustomed to live in the past, those whose blood is thrilled by Agincourt, those who feel the greatness of the classical tradition, can be so incurious as to their own spiritual origins. More and more, I think, as the changing conditions of modern society cut us off from the memory of old things; as customs die out, and property changes hands, and our language loses its virility, and even (perhaps) the power of the Empire we live in sinks in the scale of political values, men will look towards the Catholic Church, if only as the repository of long traditions, the undying, unmoved spectator of the thousand phases and fashions that have passed over our restless world. I may be wrong, but it seems to me that it is already happening; that the reaction from all this silly worship of the future is predisposing men's minds towards the Catholic claim.

And if the longevity of the Church attracts some, its worldwide diffusion has an even greater influence. It is true that Protestant controversialists have made efforts to explain away this geographical universality, insinuating that Catholicism, so far from being the religion of Europe, is only the religion of the Latin races—amongst whom, by a slight strain of ethnographical principle, it is necessary to include the Irish, the Poles, and the Hungarians. But the attempt is from the first a desperate one; Holland is two-fifths Catholic, and it was only the first world war, with its consequent territorial adjustments, that prevented the German Empire from showing, as it must have shown in a few more years, a majority of Catholic citizens. All the redistribution of Europe at and since Versailles, never conceived in a spirit friendly to Catholic interests, has failed to obscure the fact that Catholicism pervades Europe; meanwhile, recent events have done much to rob the schismatic Eastern Churches of their political solidarity and of their spiritual prestige. Catholicism is admittedly the most successful of the missionary religions, and its growth in the

New World is sufficiently attested by the alarm of its ill-wishers. Whoever wishes to find men of his own faith wherever there are men of his own species, if he does not actually wish to be a Catholic, must at least wish that he were a Catholic.

But even these glories of the Church are accidental glories. It was not immemorial, it was not worldwide, on the Day of Pentecost. There is another quality of Catholicism, more intimate and more integral, which at once repels and attracts the men of our generation—I mean the claim of the Church to authority in matters of faith and morals. This claim will, of course, occupy us throughout the present work; it has to be treated here only so far as it is, to some souls, a magnet of attraction which draws them towards the Catholic system.

When I say that the people of our time, and especially the young people of our time, want authority, I do not mean that they desire to be controlled by a coercive authority from without; only an ascetic desires that for its own sake. I mean that, in the literal and primitive sense of the word "authority", they want a warrant to authorise them in doing what they do, sanctions to justify them in behaving as they behave. This is, I believe, a characteristic symptom of our age, and very largely a post-war symptom. In normal times, there is no such demand; decent people, whatever their beliefs, are content to be guided in matters of conduct by the deliveries of their own uninstructed consciences. For, after all, the rule of man's conduct is written in his own heart. Neither Catholicism nor any other form of Christianity pretends to have a special morality of its own; religion is meant to enforce, not to supersede, the natural code of morals. (Christianity, for example, forbids suicide; but then, so did Plato.) Ideally, the perfect pagan should interpret his moral duties exactly as a Christian would.

But within the last fifty years or so an open challenge has been issued to traditional morality in matters concerning sex. A steady, ceaseless flow of literary propaganda has shaken the faith of our generation in the indissolubility of marriage, hitherto conceived as a principle of natural morality. Let anyone contrast *Jane Eyre* with the average modern novel, and he will see how far our thought has travelled. Half a century ago it was assumed, even in more or less free-thinking circles, that divorce was a disreputable subject, and that remarriage after divorce was a disqualification for respectable society. Today, such principles are maintained among Christians only with hesitation, among free-thinkers not at all.

Within the last few years a second challenge has been issued, by a less open but not less formidable propaganda, against the fruitfulness of marriage. Practices hitherto connected with the unmentioned underworld of society have found their way into the home. Once again, it is not merely a Christian principle that has been thrown overboard. It is a point over which Jewish moralists are no less definite than our own; Ovid and Juvenal, with no flicker of Christian revelation to guide them, branded the practices in question with the protest of heathen satire. It is not Christian morality, but natural morality as hitherto conceived, that has been outraged by the change of standard.

Now, the healthier part of our fellow-citizens does not want to see the effects of either propaganda carried to their logical conclusion. No decent person wants free love; no decent person wants race suicide. They live, therefore, not by principle but by a compromise between principles; they are in favour of divorce, but not of easy divorce, of small families but not of too small families. Consequently, they feel themselves responsible for the decision where exactly the line shall be drawn, within the generous limits which our legal system allows. They do not like the responsibility; who would? Who, in tampering with institutions so sacred as those of the family, would not like to feel that he had an authority behind him, a "warrant" from somewhere to ratify his behaviour? If only there were some great spiritual institution which would act, in these matters, as a sort of public conscience, guiding, from a higher point of vision, the moral choice made by the individual!

So, naturally, he feels; unfortunately, he does not feel that the views of any non-Catholic denomination are worth having, even if they are discoverable. He knows that the advice of an individual clergyman will be unofficial and inexpert. He knows, if he has followed the course of recent ecclesiastical deliberations, that representatives of Christian thought speak with an uncertain voice on such subjects. He respects our Church for having, at least, definite opinions and fixed rules. He respects it, although he disagrees with it. He thinks us far too severe in forbidding remarriage after divorce, in forbidding the artificial restriction of the family; but although he disagrees with us for the rules we have, he respects us for having rules. If only the people whom we value as advisers would give us the advice we want!

Moral hesitations chiefly affect the young; intellectual hesitations are commonly put off until they reach an age when the mind has become more reflective, and, alas! less adventurous. It is the chief tragedy of life that, whereas logically thought should precede action, in the development of man's career action precedes thought. Men who are becoming middle-aged, with families growing up and asking the eternal questions of youth, feel an ill-defined gap in their minds if they have no creed to live by, and are apt to take more notice of what the religious world is doing. They can hardly become attentive to its symptoms today without recognising, and being disturbed by, the chaos of religious sentiment which I made some attempt to describe in the foregoing chapter. They see how rapidly the fashions of thought are changing; how landmarks of tradition have been removed even within their own lifetime; they are conscious that even their own hesitating infidelities, the vogue of their youth, are becoming back numbers, as fresh doubts and fresh heresies crowd them out. The reaction from this constant flux of innovation disposes their minds, I will not say towards the idea of certitude, but towards the idea of fixity in religious beliefs. To be told, by optimistic clerical friends, that the present age is only a period of transition, and that in twenty or thirty years' time a clearer perception of spiritual truths is bound to emerge, is hardly consoling to them; they think of their grey hairs, and wonder whether they will live to see it. For that matter, the clerical optimist has been saying the same thing steadily these hundred years past. Is it wonderful if they sometimes listen, to catch the whisper of an authoritative voice?

They do not, as a rule, want authority in matters of belief for the right reason—i.e., that the whole notion of a revealed religion becomes logically impossible without it. They do not understand that the whole edifice of non-Catholic theology has always been doomed to wreck, because it never had any foundation in reason. But they do see that, here and now, there is no tradition so long established that it cannot be questioned, no doctrine so venerable that it cannot be controverted; they do see that the leaders of Protestant thought are desperately guessing at the truth, and covering up their uncertainties with equivocal phrases and sentimental whitewash. Really, the sight of it would almost make you want to be a Roman Catholic, if the Roman Catholics did not believe such impossible things. . . .

The instinct for beauty, the instinct for mystery, the instinct for naturalness, the instinct for history, the instinct for world-wide citizenship, the instinct for moral guidance, the instinct for intellectual definiteness—all these, or any of these, may make a man, do make many men, look towards the Catholic Church, if not with less reprobation, at least with more interest; if not with less ignorance, at least with more curiosity. Some wish they could become Catholics; some wish they had been born Catholics; some content themselves with saying that it must be very nice to be a Catholic. If only they could tell the first lie (as someone has put it), how easily all the rest would follow!

III

Telling the First Lie

That phrase about telling the first lie is a particularly revealing one. It reveals, not the attitude of Catholics towards religious truth, but the ignorance of non-Catholics about the religion of their fellow-countrymen.

I shall be accused, perhaps, of a sulky querulousness when I say this. It will be conjectured that I am revenging myself on those who do not agree with me by pretending that they do not understand me. But it is true, and it is a truth which becomes more luminous the more you come in contact with the public attitude towards Catholics, that the English people, when it talks about the Catholic Church, loses all sense of reality, of human possibilities. We were for so long a despised and persecuted sect, we were for so long deprived of any opportunity to explain our position, that Englishmen have come to look upon us as a race of ogres, from whom nothing natural, nothing human can be expected. They will believe anything of us, without stopping to inquire whether such beliefs are even plausible. Among half a dozen instances of this credulity, let me select one that is peculiarly striking and peculiarly well attested. At the beginning of the first world war, when it was suggested to the Government that Catholics, like their neighbours, would need an increased staff of chaplains to superintend their spiritual welfare, a Cabinet minister professed himself astonished that the ministrations of French priests would not be sufficient. And when it was pointed cut to him that these priests would find some difficulty in hearing confessions, it proved that the Cabinet minister had assumed, all his life, that Catholics made their confessions in Latin. One pictures those Irish troops, a Kennedy in every knapsack. So true is it that the English sense of realities breaks down when the habits of Catholics are in question.

By an equally grotesque illusion, most Englishmen have the idea that Catholics base *all* their religious beliefs on the authority of the Church. And if we pressed them with the difficulty, "Yes, but on what do Catholics base their belief in the authority of the Church? Do they base that on the authority of the Church too?" I suspect that most Englishmen would reply, "Of course." These people are Catholics, therefore any reason or no reason is good enough for them. They are a race apart, ogres, not men.

Let me then, to avoid further ambiguity, give a list of certain leading doctrines which no Catholic, upon a moment's reflection, could accept on the authority of the Church and on that ground alone.

1. The existence of God.

2. The fact that he has made a revelation to the world in Jesus Christ.

3. The Life (in its broad outlines), the Death, and the Resurrection of Jesus Christ.

4. The fact that our Lord founded a Church.

5. The fact that he bequeathed to that Church his own teaching office, with the guarantee (naturally) that it should not err in teaching.

6. The consequent intellectual duty of believing what the Church believes.

I do not say that these considerations are present to the mind of every Catholic, however ignorant, however stupid. I do say that these are the considerations which any Catholic teacher would put before him, if and in so far as he showed any curiosity about the matter. I would add that a glance at the Penny Catechism will disabuse any unbiased mind of the idea that the Church, even in dealing with simple folk, conceals from them the intellectual basis of their religion.

Yet the average Protestant persists in believing that the attitude of the Church towards the human intellect is adequately summed up in the phrase, familiar to us from childhood, "Open your mouth and shut your eyes." It is supposed that anybody who is brought up as a Catholic retains, without any further questioning or instruction on the point, the pious credulity with which he accepted all that his mother told him, all that the priest told him, when he was too young to think for himself. Any dawning doubts as to the sufficiency of such a motive for belief are crushed, we must suppose, with threats of hell and excommunication. This would be extraordinary enough, considering the number of Catholics there are in the world and the ample opportunities they have for being infected, in a world like ours, with the germs of unbelief. But, still more extraordinary, this Church, which has no proof of anything she says beyond her own bare assertion, is making converts, in an enlightened country like ours, at the rate of some twelve thousand in the year. How does she manage (one wonders) to play off her confidence trick with such repeated success?

This is, indeed, a phenomenon at which non-Catholics profess to feel the utmost astonishment. But it is a kind of astonishment which has grown blunted by usage; they have come to regard it as part of the order of things that their neighbours should become the victims, now and again, of this extraordinary tour de force. If they were compelled to picture to themselves the process of a conversion, they would, I suppose, conceive it something after this fashion—that the mind of the inquirer is hypnotised into acquiescence by the crafty blandishments of a designing priest; not by his arguments, for he has none, he only goes on shouting "Become a Catholic, or you will go to hell!"; not by his arguments, but by some fatal quality of fascination, which we breed, no doubt, in the seminaries. In a dazed condition, like that of the bird under the snake's eye, he assents to every formula presented to him, binds himself by every oath that is proposed to him, in one open-mouthed act of unreasoning surrender. After that, of course, pride forbids him to admit, so long as life lasts, that the choice so made was a mistaken one; besides, one knows the power these priests have. Yes, it is very curious, the power attributed to these priests. When you have had the privilege of assisting at their education for seven years, you feel that "curious" is too weak a word for it.

This is, presumably, what Protestants have in mind when they represent submission to the Church as a form of "intellectual suicide". They mean that the act of faith which a man makes in joining the Church is an act of the will (or, more properly speaking, the emotions) in which the intellect plays no part. It is an entertaining fact, familiar to all who are acquainted with the history of Protestantism, that one of the earliest and one of the fiercest controversies between the Reformation and the Old Religion was concerned precisely with this point. It was, of course, the Protestants who maintained the view that faith was an act of the will (or, more properly speaking, the emotions), with frequent allusion to the misunderstood text, "With the heart man believeth unto salvation"; whereas their Catholic opponents earned bitter hatred by insisting that the act of faith, however much directed by the will, had its seat in the intellect. Historically, Protestantism is committed to the notion that the act of faith is the mere surrender of a personality to a Personality, without parley, without deliberation, without logical motive. The true representative of Protestantism in the modern world is the Salvationist who stands up at a street corner and cries out "I am saved." It is Catholicism which insists that, ideally at least, it is the intellect which must be satisfied first, the heart afterwards.

Nor, in point of fact, has modern Protestantism any right to tax us with exalting faith at the expense of reason. It was only the other day that I read an able defence of Theism by an Anglican philosopher who appeared to demand faith of some kind as a preliminary to accepting the doctrine of God's existence. No Catholic apologist ever fell into so grotesque an error. We demand, indeed, on the part of the inquirer certain negative dispositions, as, an absence of prejudice and of frivolity, a willingness to listen and to attend, determination in carrying an argument to its logical conclusion, etc. But to demand of the inquirer any positive "will to believe" as the condition of accepting the existence of God, is to beg the whole question, to stultify the whole process of philosophical discussion.

Nobody who will take the trouble to look at any manual of Catholic apologetics will fail to understand that several of the questions most controverted today do not fall, from the Catholic point of view, under the object of faith, at least primarily. They are matters upon which we have to make up our minds beforehand, logically speaking, as a condition of making any act of faith at all. And when I say "make up our minds", I mean, not a mere decision of the will, but a satisfaction of the intellect. The existence of God, the authority of Christ, and so on, are beliefs which meet us and have to be dealt with before we get on to the act of faith at all; they are the preambles of faith, the motives of credibility. And we have to deal with them by a reasoning process, which throws the responsibility for our decision, not upon the authority of the Church, but upon our own private judgment. Every convert, when he goes under instruction, has to follow these arguments to the best of his ability. Nor is it only for the sake of converts that we insist upon this intellectual duty. A class in "apologetics" is part of the normal curriculum of a Catholic school. Catholic boys are learning to defend the existence of God at an age when you and I, reader, were dismally memorising facts abut the career of Jehoshaphat, and fleshing our teeth on the South Galatian theory.

When you have contrived to persuade him that, for Catholics, the authority of the Church in matters of faith is not a self-evident axiom, but a truth arrived at by a process of argument, the Protestant controversialist has his retort ready. "You admit, then, after all," he says, "that a man has to use his own private judgment in order to arrive at religious truth? Why, then, what is the use of authority in religion at all? I had always supposed that there was a straight issue between us, you supporting authority and I private judgment; I had always supposed that you criticised me for my presumption in searching for God by the light of my imperfect human reason; it proves, now, that you are no less guilty of such presumption than myself! Surely your reproaches are inconsistent, and your distinctions unnecessary. If you use your private judgment to establish certain cardinal points of theology, the existence of God, the authority of Christ, and so on, why may not I use my private judgment to establish not only these, but all other

points of theology—questions such as the doctrine of the
Blessed Trinity, or the Real Presence in the Eucharist? You
can hardly blame me for using the very privileges which you
have just claimed so eagerly for yourself."

I could not have imagined, if I had not heard it with my
own ears, the accent of surprise with which Protestants suddenly light upon this startling discovery, that the belief we
Catholics have in authority is based upon an act of private
judgment. How on earth could they ever suppose we taught
otherwise? I say nothing here of the grace of faith, which is
the hidden work of God in our souls. But how could the
conscious process by which we arrive at any form of the truth
begin without an act of private judgment? I may, indeed,
overcome by a kind of emotional crisis, surrender myself
unreflectively to an Influence imaginatively experienced; but
that is not Catholicism, it is Protestantism; it is "conversion"
in its crudest form. If I employ my reason at all; if I employ
my reason only so far as to say "The Church says this, and the
Church is infallible, therefore this must be true", even so I am
using private judgment; it is my own reason which draws its
conclusions from the syllogism. Reject private judgment? Of
course Catholics have never rejected private judgment; they
only profess to delimit the spheres in which private judgment
and authority have their respective parts to play.

Is it really so difficult to see that a revealed religion demands, from its very nature, a place for private judgment and
a place for authority? A place for private judgment, in determining that the revelation itself comes from God, in discov-
ering the Medium through which that revelation comes to us,
and the rule of faith by which we are enabled to determine
what is, and what is not, revealed. A place for authority to
step in, when these preliminary investigations are over, and
say "Now, be careful, for you are out of your depth here.

How many Persons subsist in the Unity of the Divine Nature, what value and what power underlie the mystery of sacramental worship, how Divine Grace acts upon the human will—these and a hundred other questions are questions which your human reason cannot investigate for itself, and upon which it can pronounce no sentence, since it moves in the natural not in the supernatural order. At this point, then, you must begin to believe by hearsay; from this point onwards you must ask, not to be convinced, but to be taught." Is it really so illogical in us, to fix the point at which our private judgment is no longer of any service? Are we really more inconsistent than the bather who steps out cautiously through the shallow water, and then, when it is breast-high, spreads out his hands to swim?

But there is a subtle and a more telling variation of the same argument. The strength of a chain, we are reminded, is that of its weakest link. We Catholics profess to establish the truths of religion by a chain of argument; this chain, then, is no stronger than the weakest link in it. How is it that we profess to hold with *absolute* certitude the revealed truths of our religion? Reasonable enough to say that *if* your Church is infallible, the doctrines which she preaches are evidently true, and capable of producing absolute certitude in the mind. But the infallibility of your Church is not a self-evident axiom; it is a proposition which you have proved, and proved it by an appeal to ordinary human reason. Is it not clear, then, that in the last resort every statement which your Church makes rests upon the validity of the arguments by which, in the first instance, you proved your Church infallible? Now, these arguments, based as they are upon human reason, do not convey absolute certitude to the mind; they may be, in your view, overwhelmingly probable; nay, they may be certain with all human certainty; but human certainty is not *absolute* certainty.

There is always a possible margin of error. You cannot prove the existence of God, the authority of Christ, or his commission to his Church, beyond all possibility of doubt; how then can you suppose that you have proved beyond all possibility of doubt the statements which you receive on the Church's authority?

To escape this dilemma, Catholic apologists have frequently used a metaphor which seems to me, I confess, singularly unfortunate. They tell us that the motives of credibility by which we establish the divine origin of the Church, and her teaching office, are like the scaffolding which is put up while a building is being erected; once the building operations are complete, the scaffolding is unnecessary; it has served its turn, and we pay it no further attention. Now, theologically speaking, that metaphor will pass well enough; they mean that the true motive of our belief, seen on its supernatural side, is the infallible veracity of God in his revelation. But for purposes of apologetic, we shall employ such a metaphor in vain. Our critics will not be slow to point out that we erect a building inside the scaffolding, not on the top of the scaffolding; and if we did erect a building on the top of our scaffolding, we could not take the scaffolding away without letting the building fall to the ground. Our own parable has been turned against us.

It will be better to avoid the metaphor, and to keep in mind the distinction just mentioned. The motives of credibility, satisfying his intellect, bring the inquirer up to the point of making the act of faith. That act recognises God's authority in the Church's teaching; and the absolute nature of his authority does make all the difference to the kind of certitude with which, thenceforward, he holds the truths of Catholic doctrine. But this is inherent in the act of faith, not in the chain of proof by which the Catholic claim is established. Having made the act of faith, he cannot produce more or better arguments to convince his neighbour than he could have produced before. Apologetically, then, revealed truths have no higher certitude than the arguments by which the fact of revelation is established. The revealed proposition that there are Three Persons in the Blessed Trinity is not, apologetically, more certain than the statement (established in the first instance by private judgment) that our Lord left the charisma of infallibility to his Church.

The Catholic claim does not profess to be based on a mathematical certainty. The proposition "Things which are equal to the same thing are equal to one another" is evident in the sense that the contrary proposition is unthinkable. The proposition "Jesus of Nazareth suffered under Pontius Pilate" is not evident in that sense; the contrary proposition, in this case, does not defy our thought. In historical statements (and every revealed religion must depend, in the last resort, upon an historical statement) the highest kind of certainty you can attain is that which excludes reasonable doubt. That is the kind of proof which Catholicism claims for those preliminary considerations which it calls "the motives of credibility". And consequently no point of Catholic doctrine can claim anything better than this historical kind of proof. The absolute certainty with which we believe the teaching of the Church comes to us from the supernatural grace of faith, which transforms our reasoned conviction into a higher quality— the water, as at Cana, is turned into wine. But *for apologetic purposes* a reasoned conviction is all we can offer to our neighbours; and it is this reasoned conviction which the present thesis attempts to maintain.

It will be observed that those Platonic admirers of the Catholic system to whom I referred in the last chapter—the people who "wish they were Catholics" without having in fact any intention of becoming Catholics—are usually guilty of an utter misconception. They imagine that the Catholic Church is asking them to make a leap in the dark; and they feel, sometimes, as if they would like to make that leap, or rather, to have made it, because it would save them the trouble of any intellectual effort. If only they could be trepanned into the Church, if only they could be shanghaied on board the Ark of Peter, the passage would quite possibly (they feel) be a pleasant one. But the Church is not asking them to take any such sudden leap—will not allow them, in fact, to assume rights of membership until they have been through a course of intellectual instruction. It is their duty to satisfy their own minds, proportionately to their general level of mental culture, about God's existence, the authority of Christ, etc., before they can expect the grace of faith to come to them.

A full statement of Catholic belief may, of course, be made without entering into apologetic considerations at all. The question "What do you Catholics teach?" may be interpreted as a demand, inspired by enlightened curiosity, to have the revealed doctrines which we inculcate set forth in an orderly scheme. But the reader of such a document, unless he is himself a Catholic or at least a catechumen, holds these doctrines at arm's length as he considers them, regards them merely as an exposé of his neighbours' religious psychology; they have not, for him, the interest of an appeal or a challenge. I am fully conscious how difficult it is for anyone to make such an appeal, such a challenge successfully; fully conscious that my own qualifications for the task are at best those of an amateur, not those of a specialist. But I am writing in the hope, not merely of informing the reader, but of persuading him, or at least of contributing to that end. Consequently, I must take nothing for granted; I must adopt for my model the author whom Horace condemned for beginning his epic of Troy with the story of Leda's egg; I must assume that the reader has an open mind even on the question whether God exists or no.

I am the more encouraged to take this course by the fact that in our day many intelligent people who profess themselves Theists hold their beliefs precariously and unreflectively, without troubling to inquire what they involve; nay, that Christians themselves, from a lack of systematic instruction, often misconceive the Nature of the God whom their own theology preaches, and are half-way towards pantheism without knowing it. It will do no harm to test each link in the chain of Christian apologetic, be the hand that wields the hammer never so unworkmanlike.

IV

The God Who Hides Himself

Philosophers have continually been exercised by the question whether our knowledge of God is a direct or a derived knowledge; whether the idea of God is in some way native to the mind, or whether we arrive at it through our knowledge of other things, his creatures. The mystical temperament, which has a strong influence on the outlook of Protestant theologians, is naturally disposed to claim, if the claim can in any way be justified, that our knowledge of God is direct. For it is the instinct of the mystic to reject, as far as possible, all interference, all mediation, between God and the soul.

The simplest, the most plausible of all these theories is Traditionalism. As a matter of observation, it is plainly true that the origin from which your knowledge of God is derived, or mine, is the assurance given to us in infancy by our mothers or those who were responsible for our education. What if this should be not only the origin, but the justification of the concept? Adam, we must suppose, had in some way an experimental knowledge of God's existence. Did not he, in the strength of that knowledge, make Theists of his sons, and they of theirs, and so on down the whole series of history, until at last the information came to our mothers, and through them to us? The evidence we have, in that case, for the existence of God is a tradition, perpetuated through the long course of human history, and resting in the last resort on the testimony of men who had walked with God, who had had first-hand knowledge of the facts,

Or, failing that, there is a possible refuge in Fideism. After all, religion is concerned with the supernatural order, which altogether transcends ours; why should there not be a special, supernatural revelation to man which enables him to apprehend the existence of God; made, if you will, before he is yet old enough to be conscious of the fact? Is it not, perhaps, the best account we can give of this persistent human belief in a Deity, to suppose that there is a special faculty implanted in all of us at birth, but obscured in some of us by faults of training or of character, which apprehends God by a simple act, unintellectual because it is supra-intellectual?

One philosopher at least, Descartes, would go further than this, and claim that for this purpose no supernatural revelation was needed. The thinking mind, according to his analysis, was primarily conscious of two clear and distinct ideas, itself and God. Outward things, the phenomena of sense, were only mirrored for it through the medium of its own consciousness; but the two facts of its own existence and God's were guaranteed to it antecedently to any reasoning whatsoever. At the very basis of all our thought lay the perception of a God who was responsible for implanting in us the ideas with which our thought is concerned; his non-existence was worse than unthinkable, it would destroy the very possibility of all knowledge. You must believe in God in order to believe in anything at all.

This was at the dawn of Idealism; but a theory not altogether dissimilar had found patronage even in the scholastic age—I mean the "Ontological proof" which is usually connected with the name of St. Anselm. The idea of God was necessarily one of supreme Perfection; it was impossible to associate the notion of any fault or defect with the idea of God. But the notion of non-existence is the notion of a fault or defect—indeed, a very considerable one. Therefore it is impossible to associate the notion of non-existence with the idea of God. Therefore it is unthinkable that God should not exist; therefore God exists.

This attempt to prove the existence of God, or to declare the proof of it unnecessary, without reference to the effects of his power which we experience in his visible creation, is a permanent temptation to the human mind. Intellects as far removed from one another as those of Anselm, Descartes, and de Bonald have undertaken it, and it is probable that they will never lack successors. Protestant thought, in our day, is much wedded not to these but to similar speculations. Thus, you will seldom read any piece of non-Catholic apologetic without coming across some reference to man's sense of his need for God, or man's notion of holiness, a notion which can only be perfectly realised in God. The implication of all such language is that it is possible to argue directly from the existence of concepts in our own mind to the existence of real objects, to which those concepts correspond.

The Catholic Church discountenances all such methods of approach to the subject; some of them, at the Vatican Council, she has actually condemned. She discountenances them, at least, if and in so far as they claim to be the sole or the main argument for the existence of God. The main, if not the sole, argument for the existence of God—so she holds, and has always held—is the argument which proves the Unseen from the seen, the existence of the Creator from his visible effects in Creation.

All these efforts at the solution of the problem really depend for their plausibility on a postulate which we do not grant—namely, that it would have been impossible for the human race to infer God's existence from his creatures. If this were true, then it might be argued that the notion of God must be an idea directly communicated to our minds. Such an argument is perfectly valid if applied to our sense of right and wrong; it must be native to the mind, because there is nothing outside ourselves which could possibly have suggested such a notion to us. But this is a simple idea, directly entertained; whereas the idea of God is a composite idea, and the attributes which we associate with it, power, wisdom, etc., are derived from our own experience. "If there had been no God," said Napoleon, "it would have been necessary to invent him"—at least, we may say it would have been *possible* to invent him. Thus the fact that the idea of God is conceived by our minds does not *necessarily* mean that it is inborn in us, or that it is directly communicated to us by some supernatural light.

The supposition is an unnecessary one, and now, what has it to say for itself? If it were true, as Descartes held, that the idea of God was a clear and distinct idea, like that of our own existence, why is it that there are so few fools in the world who doubt their own existence, so many who say "there is no God"? If the existence of God was one of the first principles of all our mental process, then the contrary idea, that there is no God, should be unthinkable—but is it unthinkable? People think it every day. "But at least," St. Anselm would retort, "it is impossible to think of an imperfect God, and therefore it is impossible to think of a non-existent God." To which the atheist replies with some justice that, since God does not exist, it is not necessary to think about him at all. You cannot argue from the ideal to the real order of things.

The apologist is on safer ground if he leaves the arena of philosophy altogether, and maintains that the notion of God, so far from being innate in our minds, is something supernaturally implanted in them by a kind of direct revelation. That some such revelation was made to our first parents, we have no ground for disputing; but it would need a robust faith in us to accept so momentous a doctrine on the remote authority of our first parents, even if popular science would give us leave to suppose that we had any. Can we really be certain that in so many centuries of transmission the revelation has remained intact—that the tale has not lost in the telling? On the other hand, Fideism would have us believe that such a direct revelation is made not once for all to the human race, but to each individual soul. Is it? The argument is surely one of those which admit of no refutation and produce no conviction. It is impossible to disprove the assertion that a direct revelation was made to us at a time of life from which no memories remain to us; but equally it is impossible to prove it. And if some other account can be given of the means by which the race or the individual arrives at the knowledge of God, surely this rather desperate hypothesis is best left in the limbo of mere conjecture.

I know there is a fashion amongst modern apologists to write as if man possessed a religious sense, comparable to his sense of music. This sense (so the argument runs) is most highly developed in the saint, the mystic, who is the real artist, the real connoisseur; in most men it is much less developed; in some it is hardly developed at all. Not that anyone (God forbid!) can be born absolutely tone-deaf to the airs of this heavenly music; but, through lack of development, the talent is nearly buried; there is no response, or practically no response, made by such a soul to the Divine voice within. The spiritual man discerns spiritual things; he cannot explain to you what his experiences are, or even how he knows that they are real, any more than the musical expert can explain his emotional experiences to the mere groundling. But he knows; he has had an unmistakable experience of God's Presence; it does not become us, the ignorant amateurs, to dispute his judgment. We can only trust to his higher instincts; and hope that we, too, perhaps, may be privileged to hear now and again some echo of the strains that ravish him.

For the life of me I could never understand how far such authors mean their metaphor to be pressed. Is it really contended that we can argue from a state of mind to an objective reality which lies behind it? If a musical enthusiast, after listening to some rare but gay piece, should tell me that as he listened he could actually see elves and gnomes dancing before his eyes, I should be perfectly prepared to reverence both his own superior sensitiveness to musical impressions, and the subtle power of the art which could evoke such an imaginative experience. I should not suppose that elves or gnomes had been present, unseen to myself. And I confess that if I lacked the sense of religion quite so thoroughly as I lack that of music, the disclosures of the mystic would leave me in very much the same position. I might feel the mystic to be of a spiritual calibre infinitely superior to my own; I might bestow my admiration on those methods of contemplative prayer which enabled him to achieve his sense of a Divine Presence, his sense of Union. But I should not for that reason be inclined to believe in the objective existence of God, his Angels, or his Saints, if I did not share those beliefs already.

I do not know if I am wholly removed from the generality of mankind in holding such sentiments; but this type of argument seems to me both logically unsound and theologically perilous. And the nerve of the fallacy lies, I think, in the use of the word "experience". When we are asked to let ourselves be guided by the experiences of another in matters of common human importance, we acquiesce (if we do acquiesce) because the experiences in question are such as might have fallen to our lot instead of his; we have eyes, ears, and the other senses corresponding to his. And we can take the measure of his faculties from our own; if he says he saw a thing, we can relate that to our own experience of sight; if he says he heard a thing, we can relate it to our own sense of hearing. But if a man talks to us of "experiences" in which the faculties of outward sensation played no part, we are no longer in a position to sample those experiences for ourselves by proxy; we have no apparatus for sharing them with him. Where an experience of the outward senses is concerned, we are ready, from the analogy of our own experience, to believe that there was "something there". But when the alleged experience has been apprehended through the use of spiritual faculties which we either do not possess or do not use, our confidence in the "something there" necessarily evaporates. Which is, I suppose, why the Church tells us that a private revelation may be such as to demand credence from the soul which experiences it, but can never, of itself, demand credence from other people.

Nevertheless the moderns, in their desire for an easy short cut to the proof of God's existence, are learning to rest more and more weight on this tenuous argument—as I think, fatally. In the same way, they press for more than it is worth the argument, impressive enough in itself, that, when all is said and done, most people do believe in God. Buddhism, Hinduism, paganism have at least theologies of their own; Jewry and Islam acknowledge, no less than Christendom, one God who is both transcendent and omnipotent. In England itself, for all the decline of official Christianity which we were considering three chapters back, how much is there of positive atheism? Nor is the appeal to history less impressive; with a thousand strange vagaries of presentation, humanity has nearly always, nearly everywhere, attested its belief in the existence of unseen Powers; atheism nearly always, nearly everywhere, has been the reaction of a minority, a protest defying the popular instinct. Must there not, argues the apologist, be something in this popular certainty? Have we not been taught to remember that there is no smoke without fire? We can hardly account for this vast conspiracy of mankind, determined to bow down before some august Power, conceived as intelligent and present to the worshipper; we can hardly account for the satisfaction of man's highest instincts through such commerce with the Unseen, except on the supposition (which, after all, cannot be disproved) that the God so worshipped under a thousand forms and in a thousand manners does really exist.

This contention, put in its most naked form, means that each of us ought to believe in God because all the others do—an arrangement not differing much in principle from the economics of that famous country, whose inhabitants lived by taking in one another's washing. Once more we must insist, you cannot argue from a mere state of mind to an objective reality which that state of mind appears to presuppose. If indeed there were no way of accounting for this strange idea having got into so many people's heads, then the mere fact of its prevalence might make us suspect that there was something in it. But, as we shall see presently, it is possible to give some account of how the idea of God comes into men's minds. Or again, if each human being independently discovered the idea of God for himself, we might hesitate to ascribe the phenomenon to mere coincidence. But the doctrine of God's existence is one that is taught to childhood, one that is often bound up, superstitiously, with national hopes, with social ordinances. Even if there were no God, it is probable enough that many people would believe in his existence; it would not be more surprising than the belief in luck, for example, or the belief in omens.

No, the true lesson of this widespread and obstinate Theism among our fellow-men is a slightly different one. The fact that so many men believe in a God ought to set us wondering whether there are not, perhaps, reasons for such a belief, to which we have not hitherto devoted sufficient attention; or perhaps reasons which we scorned to look into, because we had vaguely been given to understand that they were out of date and unfashionable. Mankind's belief in God is a rebuke to, and a condemnation of, the careless atheist. For it is the height of rashness or of pride to assume without investigation that so large a part of the race is giving credit to an illusion, for the existence of which no rational grounds can be assigned.

In a word, the existence of religion is a challenge to us to consider eagerly whether there are not grounds for believing in God's existence, philosophical grounds which will be as cogent for us as they have been for others. When I say "philosophical", I do not mean that it is the duty of the bushman or of the charcoal-burner to go through a series of carefully-arranged scholastic syllogisms. I mean that there exists among mankind a sort of rough, common-sense metaphysic which demands as its first postulate the existence of a divine principle in things. It can be refined, it can be reduced to terms, by the nice ratiocinations of the philosopher; it is equally valid (we hold) whether as it presents itself to the charcoal-burner or as it presents itself to the sage.

The schoolmen, whose method has left its stamp upon all subsequent Catholic apologetics, distinguished five avenues of approach by which we infer, from the conditions of our outward experience, the existence of a God.

1. In all motion, or rather, as we should say, in all change, you can separate two elements, active and passive, that which is changed and that which changes it. But, in our experience, the agent in such change is not self-determined, but determined in its turn by some higher agent. Can this process go on *ad infinitum*? No, for an infinite series of agents, none of them self-determined, would not give us the finality which thought demands; there must be, at the beginning of the series, however long, an Agent who is self-determined, who is the ultimate Agent in the whole cycle of changes that proceeds from him.

2. Similarly, in our experience every event is determined by a cause. But that cause in its turn is itself an event determined by a cause. An infinite series of causes would give no explanation of how the causation ever began. There must therefore be an uncaused Cause, which is the ultimate Cause of the whole nexus of events which proceeds from it.

3. In our experience, we find nothing which exists in its own right; everything depends for its existence on something else. This is plain in the case of the organised individual; for plants, animals, etc., are born, live, and die; that is to say, their existence is only contingent, not necessary—it depends on conditions outside itself. Now, although the whole sum of matter does not, in our experience, increase or diminish, we cannot think of it as existing necessarily—it is just *there*. Its existence, then, must depend on something outside itself— something which exists necessarily, of its own right. That Something we call God.

4. In our experience, there are various degrees of natural perfection. But the existence of the good and the better implies the existence of a Best; for (according to Plato's system of thought) this Best is itself the cause and the explanation of all good. But this Best is not found in our earthly

experience, therefore it must lie beyond our earthly experience; and it is this Best which we call God.

5. Everywhere in Nature we observe the effects of order and system. If blind chance ruled everything, this prevalence of order would be inexplicable; it would be a stupendous coincidence. Order can only be conceived as the expression of a Mind; and, though our mind appreciates the existence of order in the world, it is not our mind which has introduced it there. There must therefore exist outside our experience, a Mind of which this order is the expression; and that Mind we call God.

It is often objected that this analysis of the facts is unnecessarily itemised; it repeats the same argument under different forms. For the purposes of the plain man, it may perhaps be admitted that the first three of these arguments are not readily distinguishable. He apprehends God in his Creation, first as all-powerful and the source of all power (1, 2, and 3); then as all-good and the source of all goodness (4); then as all-wise and the source of all wisdom (5). For all the changes that have swept over Europe since the twelfth century, he has not been bullied out of his conviction.

It is true, the little books of popular science which he reads in his corner of the railway train, talk as if all this process of thought were antiquated; as if something had happened in the meantime which made Creation self-explanatory without the postulate of a Creator. Their cocksure implications affect him like briers that flick a man across the face without turning him aside from his direction. They tell him that matter is indestructible, not elucidating their meaning, which is that Man is incapable of destroying it; but even so he will not believe that matter has existed, for no particular reason, from all eternity; or that, stranger still, it brought itself into existence. They write of Force with a capital F, or Energy with a capital E, as if we had somehow managed to deify those conceptions. But he knows that whereas motion is a fact that can be observed, force is a concept with which he is only acquainted through his experience as a living creature; it is a function of life, and the forces of Nature (as they are called), over which neither man nor beast exercises any control, must be functions of a Life which is outside experience itself. They write as if Science had made the problem of existence simpler by explaining the causes of things hitherto unexplained—by showing us that disease is due to the action of microbes, or that lightning comes from the electricity in the atmosphere. But he knows that all this only puts the question a stage further back; that he is still at liberty to ask what caused the microbes, what caused the electricity. The thought of an infinite series, whether of causes or of agents, is no more attractive to him than to St. Thomas.

Of course, it is possible to avoid all these speculations with a bovine murmur of "I don't know nothing about that." But this is to give up the riddle, and to give it up, not because you cannot find the answer, but because you have found the answer, and have found it to be unpalatable. The lines of our experience, even in the natural world outside us, converge towards one point, presuppose a Creator who has necessary existence, a Prime Mover, a First Cause. But the created universe points to the existence not merely of an uncreated Power, but of an uncreated Mind.

This argument from the order and systems to be found in Creation is not synonymous with the argument from design; the argument from design, in the narrow sense, is a department or application of the main thesis. Design implies the adaptation of means to ends; and it used to be confidently urged that there was one end which the Creator clearly had in view, the preservation of species, and one plain proof of his purposive working, namely, the nice proportion between the instincts or endowments of the various animal species and the environment in which they had to live. The warm coats of the Arctic animals, the differences of strength, speed, and cunning which enable the hunter and the hunted to live together without the extermination of either—these would be instances in point; modern research has given us still more salient instances of the same principle, such as the protective mimicry which renders a butterfly or a nest of eggs indistinguishable from its surroundings. Was it not a Mind which had so proportioned means to ends?

The argument was a dangerous one, so stated. It took no account of the animal species which have in fact become extinct; it presupposed, also, the fixity of animal types. God's mercy, doubtless, is over all his works, but we are in no position to apply teleological criticism to its exercise and to decide on what principle the wart-hog has survived while the dodo has become extinct. In this precise form, then, the argument from order has suffered badly. But the argument from order, as the schoolmen conceived it, was and is a much wider and less questionable consideration. It is not merely in the adaptation of means to ends, but in the reign of law throughout the whole field of Nature, that we find evidence of a creative Intelligence. By a curious trick of human vanity, we describe a newly-discovered principle in Nature as So-and-so's Law, Boyle's, or Newton's, or Tyndall's, as if the discoverer were himself the legislator. I am not grudging honour to the pioneers of research; I am only commenting on an oddity of phrase. Surely, when a thing is unexpectedly found, we congratulate the person who has found it, but our next question is inevitably, "Who put it there?" And, if there are laws in Nature to be discovered, it is but natural to ask the same question, "Who put them there?" If it needs a mind to discover them, did it not need a Mind to devise them? If the whole of our experience is not a phantasmagoria of unrelated facts, if water does not flow uphill, and gases do not double in volume when the pressure on them is doubled, who was it willed that the thing should be so? Not we assuredly; not Boyle, not Newton. Not blind Chance, for there is a limit to coincidence. Not "Nature", for there is no such person; she is only an abstraction. What hypothesis is left to us except that of an ordering Mind? Instinctively we speak of a law when we find a natural principle; and have we no right to argue from a law to a Legislator?

I know that to superior persons all this will sound very naïve. But it is easy to suspect simplicity in your opponent's mind, when the simplicity really lies in the facts. There are thoughts so obvious that we are apt not to reflect upon them, so familiar that we are in danger of forgetting them.

So far we have been dealing with the evidences for God's existence which are concerned with outward nature, not with the inner life of man. The argument from perfection adduced by the schoolmen is not the modern argument from moral perfection. The plain man would probably conceive the relations between God and man in the moral sphere with more of directness, more of concreteness. He would tell us that the voice of conscience was a voice not his own; whose then can it be, if it be not Divine? Or he would tell us, in Kant's vein, that the sense of moral duty is the sense of an obligation imposed upon us by a sovereignty outside ourselves—whose sovereignty, if not God's? Or he would tell us that the sense of compunction which he feels when he has done wrong is not to be explained away as mere disappointment with himself; it carries with it the sense that he has defied a power above himself—whose power, if it be not God's? To each his own appeal; there is little need to dwell on this side of the argument; for probably everyone who has the least hankerings after Theism feels the force of it in one form or another. Otherwise I would ask space to argue that the scholastic form of it has a special value, as the truest both to the philosophic and to the devotional instinct.

I have made no attempt in this chapter to deal with the objections which will present themselves to minds influenced by the more intimate doubts of Idealism. I have been forced to assume, what the schoolmen assumed, and most ordinary people assume, that our thought is an instrument adequate to the cognition of objective reality. Still less have I attempted to anticipate the rejoiners of the Pragmatist—who, it seems to me, above all men should wish to be a Catholic, and above all men will find it difficult to become one. I have merely indicated the course which Catholic apologetic takes in this fundamental matter, trusting that the inquirer, if his doubts begin so early in the process, will find access to more lucid and more copious expositions than mine.

V

The Catholic Notion of God

If the arguments adduced in the foregoing chapter are valid, they commit us not only to a belief in the Existence of God, but to certain views as to his Nature. I do not mean to discuss or even enumerate here, as a text-book of theology would, the various Attributes of God, for fear of unduly crowding the canvas. It is enough for our present purposes to insist that the God who is postulated by a consideration of his works in Nature must be a transcendent God, an omnipotent God, and a personal God. The very nerve of our contention is that the material world which meets us in our experience does not provide the explanation of its own existence, or of the forces which control it, or of the laws which govern it; that the explanation, consequently, must be looked for in something that is outside and beyond itself. Our thought can only be satisfied by the existence of some necessary Being, to which all this contingent existence around us, the world of creation, is secondary, and upon which it depends.

Upon which, or rather, upon whom. We must always explain the lower in terms of the higher, not the higher in terms of the lower. And the highest form of existence of which we have any experience is Spirit. Man finds himself possessed of this apparently unique privilege, that he can become the object of his own thought. He can focus his attention, not merely upon things outside himself, but upon himself the thinker, upon himself thinking. Adam must have had many strange experiences when he woke in Paradise, but none stranger than that of meeting himself. The difference between this self-consciousness and mere consciousness is as real, as vital, as the difference between consciousness itself and mere life, or the difference between life and mere existence. This spiritual principle, this self-conscious life within man, is not accounted for (still less explained) by his needs as a mere citizen of the natural creation. It is something altogether outside the scheme of ordinary organic life; it exists for its own sake, and must therefore be regarded as a higher order of existence. It is to this higher order of existence, naturally, that he refers that highest of all possible existences which he calls by the name of God.

It has been a favourite taunt of the unbeliever, from Xenophanes down to Rupert Brooke, that if horses had conceived of theology, they would have imagined God like themselves, if fishes had invented a theology, they would have imagined God like themselves. The criticism is one of those which miss the mark so completely as to provide their own refutation. For the fact is that man is superior to horses and fishes in one point, namely, his self-consciousness, his spiritual life; and it is precisely in virtue of that spiritual quality, and of that alone, that he has dared to conceive of God as like to himself. He conceives of God not as a Big Man, but as a Great Spirit, lacking precisely those features of inferiority which link man, in his dual nature, to the brutes. Man's soul, which in memory, in intellect, and in will stands outside of and superior to the accidents of his mortality, is the only mirror he finds in Nature of that pure Act, that tireless Energy which is God.

And if God be Spirit, then he is a personal God. For all our experience of spirit, all our evidence for its existence, rests upon the first-hand consciousness which each man has of himself, and second-hand indications which point to the existence of a similar consciousness in his neighbour. Each spirit, as it is given to us in our experience, is a lonely point of conscious existence. Matter, as we know it, may enter into various combinations and assume various forms; we do not meet with spirit, we only meet with spirits. And the notion that God is, not *a* Spirit, but the totality of existing spirits and nothing more; the notion that he is Spirit and not *a* Spirit is pure mythology. It overlooks that individuality, that incommunicableness, which belongs to all spirits in our experience. It is not suggested, of course, that the Being who created us is subject to all the limitations which our minds may happen to associate with the word "personality". But in thinking of God as a Spirit, we cannot rule out the idea of conscious individuality; for that idea is essential to our whole conception of a spiritual nature.

We must not conceal from ourselves the fact that in so defining the Nature of God as transcendent, omnipotent, and personal, we have parted company with a great number of the more religiously affected of mankind. We have said nothing, so far, which could not be echoed by a Jew or by a Mohammedan. But we have quarrelled, already, with that pantheistic conception of the Divine Being which has had such a profound influence on other religions of the East.

The vice of pantheism is that its theology takes Life, not Spirit, as its point of departure. Dichotomising the world (wrongly) into matter and life, the pantheist assumes that the animal organism is the mirror of the universe. As, in the animal, matter finds a principle of life to organise it, so the whole sum of matter in existence must have a Life to organise it; a Life which is the summing up of all the life (vegetable or animal) which exists. This Life is God; God is to the world what the soul (in the widest sense) is to the body. Thus, on the one hand, the pantheist theology contrives to give an explanation of existence which is no explanation at all; for the totality of our experience plus a World-Soul does not, by reason of the addition, provide any account of how or why it came into existence. And on the other hand it encumbers our thought with the concept of a God who is no God; who is, indeed, but an abstraction, as animal life divorced from matter is an abstraction; who can neither affect our destinies, nor prescribe our conduct, nor claim our worship; impotent, unmoral, and only demanding by courtesy the typographical compliment of a capital G.

So sharply is the God whom we Catholics worship—we Catholics, with the Jews and the Mohammedans—divided from the notion of deity which has syncretised, spiritualised, or superseded the many-headed monsters of the pagan East. Is the God of modern Protestantism so clearly marked off from his Oriental counterpart? I confess that I entertain acute and growing misgivings on this point. The tendency of Protestantism, as I suggested in the last chapter, is to find its evidence of God's existence rather in some supposed instinct or intuition than in any inference from premises grounded in experience. But such methods of proof, even granted their validity, would only warrant us in accepting the fact of his existence, without telling us anything about his Nature. Most men believe in God; yes, but then a very large percentage of them are pantheists of one shade or another; the common belief of mankind does not, then, proclaim the existence of a Deity who is transcendent.

There is in man's nature an itch for worship, an instinct for religion; yes, but what sort of religion? Why should not Buddhism (for example) satisfy the craving? Mystics have had direct experience of God's Presence; it behoves us, then, to trust their experience rather than our own earth-bound imaginations—yes, but which mystics? The Christian or the Buddhist mystics? Unless we are prepared to fall back on the doctrine of Descartes and Berkeley, who would make God immediately responsible for those ideas through which alone we come in contact with any outside reality, it seems to me that all "direct" proofs of God's existence yield only a blank formula, which we have no intellectual apparatus for filling in.

What kind of God, then, does Protestantism mean to propose for our worship? Our Idealist philosophers, still mournfully chewing the cud of Hegelianism, have no assurance to offer, either that God is omnipotent, or in what sense he is personal. There remains only the moral argument to distinguish Protestantism in its more adventurous forms from the cruder forms of pantheism. Doubtless it will always be held, at least in the Western Hemisphere, that the Supreme Being, however conceived, must be the summing-up of all those aspirations towards goodness which our own moral experience teaches us to indulge. But is such a God necessarily the Judge of living and dead? Is it permissible to pray to him, in the sense of asking for favours which he can grant? Has he the Attributes of the God whom Jesus of Nazareth preached, and claimed, apparently, to reveal? Surely it is time that Protestant theologians should consider seriously the very fundamentals of their thought; and this question not least, What do we know of God's Nature; and on what basis of thought does that knowledge rest? For in this matter the ideas of their half-hearted supporters are lamentably incoherent; and such hesitation may easily lend a handle, before long, to the propaganda of Theosophy.

The doctrine of God's Omnipotence carries with it a further admission which will be of considerable importance in succeeding chapters—I mean, the permanent possibility of miracle. If the laws of the natural creation are not an expression of God's Nature, as the pantheist would hold, but merely of his Will, it follows that he is at liberty, if he will, to suspend their action; or rather, to supersede their action by that of higher laws which have not been made known to us. It is only reasonable—would that it were as common as it is reasonable—to have a clear notion as to the possibility of miracles happening, before we come to estimate the evidence, debatable in itself as all historical evidence must be, which claims that miracles have actually occurred in history.

A century and a half ago, it would have been necessary to investigate carefully, in this connection, the philosophic system known as Deism. It was but natural that the triumphs of mechanical science in the eighteenth century should impose on men's minds the idea of mechanism; it was but natural that the Christian apologetic of the period should reflect this idea in its turn. Deism asserts strongly the first two scholastic proofs of God's existence, while neglecting the third. If we think of God merely as the First Cause and the Prime Mover, it is not necessary to think of him as influencing the course of the natural Creation here and now. You may think of him, instead, at some moment in the infinitely remote past, fashioning a world, giving it laws, physical and biological, to guide its movements, and then turning it adrift, like a ship with its tiller lashed, to reach its inevitable and foreseen destiny. Paley's metaphor of the watch once for all wound up is, of course, the classic illustration of this Deist conception. It represents God as having made the universe, but not as guiding it from moment to moment, still less as actually holding it in being. Such a system was considerably embarrassed to find room for the possibility of miracle. To intrude miracle upon a cosmos so governed would have been to put a spoke in the wheels of the machine, with consequences fatally disturbing to the scheme of the whole.

Deism, nowadays, is cited only as a vagary of the past; it has few, if any, living supporters. It is hardly necessary, then, to remind the reader that laws do not carry themselves out; they are principles which need an executive to enforce them; and to conceive the laws of Nature as acting on their own initiative, independently of God's concurrence, is to personify those laws, if not actually to deify them. The Catholic notion of God's relation to the universe is summed up once for all in our Lord's statement that no sparrow can fall to the ground without our Heavenly Father; there can be no event, however insignificant, however apparently fortuitous, however cruel in its bearing on the individual, which does not demand, here and now, the concurrence of the Divine Power. I do not mean that Catholic thought bases this belief on our Lord's utterance; it belongs to natural, not to revealed theology. God alone exists necessarily; our existence is contingent, depends, that is to say, from moment to moment upon an exercise of his will; he has not left the reins, he has not lashed the tiller; he works not *by means of* the laws, but only according to the laws, which he has laid down for himself in determining the governance of his creatures.

It will easily be seen that, once this view of the Divine economy is grasped, there can be no further talk of ruling out miracles on the ground of impossibility. It is still open to the objector to say that it would be inconsistent with our idea of God's dignity to imagine him as interfering with his own laws; or that it would be a criticism on those laws themselves to suppose they could ever need to be suspended in favour of an individual need. Such objections we shall have to meet later; for the present, it is enough to point out that miracles, so far as their possibility is concerned, do fit into the scheme of things. Indeed, to describe God as Almighty is to admit that miracles are possible. The difficulty, it may even be said, for our human imaginations is to understand the fall of the sparrow rather than to understand the feeding of the Five Thousand. For in the fall of the sparrow, as in the feeding of the multitude, the Divine Power is at work; only in this case the concurrence of God as the Primary Cause with those secondary "causes", which we are apt to imagine as complete in themselves, is a thing as baffling to the imagination as it is necessary to thought.

We have been considering only the first article of the Creed which Catholics and Protestants alike recognise, "I believe in God the Father Almighty." It will be seen that the outline of the Catholic system is already beginning to take shape on the canvas; it begins already to stand out in relief, not only as against the pantheistic religions of the East, never attractive to our fellow-countrymen, but against much vagueness and indecision which is to be read or to be suspected in non-Catholic works of theology. It is not that Protestantism, in its official formularies, finds or has ever found cause of disagreement with us in such fundamental matters as these. But I shall be very much surprised if the arguments which I have adduced, and the conclusions I have inferred from them, in this and the preceding chapter, do not cause some of my clerical critics to hold up their hands already at the intransigence, the medievalism of the thought which is here represented. The Catholic notion of God ought not to be distinct from the Protestant notion of God, but I fear that in practice a shadow of difference is already discernible between them. If this is so, it must be attributed, first, to the departmentalism, the absence of system, which reigns among non-Catholic theologians; partly to the spirit of unauthorised adventure which makes them start out gaily in pursuit of some novel thesis; partly to the extreme incuriosity with which the average worshipper regards all details of doctrine. I wish I could think that my estimate of the situation was exaggerated, and my forebodings of the future a scruple.

VI

The Seed-Ground of Revelation

It would be wholly preposterous to approach the next stage in
the argument for Catholicism—I mean the emergence of the
Christian revelation—without paying some attention to the
Providential history (so we reckon it) of the Jewish people.
Circumstances have not been wanting to bring Judaism and
Christendom into conflict; and the scars of that conflict remain. But Judaism and Catholicism have subtle qualities in
common; and I fancy that a Jewish convert enters the Church
more naturally and more simply than a Protestant would; he
has less of prejudice and of scruple to live down; his new
beliefs are a continuation rather than a correction of the old.
And small wonder; for the foundation upon which Christian
thought is based is not mere Theism, but Theism cast in a
particular mould by the influence of Jewish thought.

We must not, of course, at this stage in the proceedings,
talk of Old Testament literature as if it possessed any quality of
inspiration, in the ecclesiastical sense of the term. That admission will be made much later on, for it is an admission which
we accept only on the authority of the Church. For the
present, we must accord to the Old Testament only that
relative and guarded confidence which we should accord to

Herodotus or to Livy. Nor do I propose to write here as if any certainty had yet been attained as to the dates at which the various Old Testament books were compiled. A century of irresponsible criticism, conducted on both sides of the North Sea by a handful of confident scholars, has reached various "conclusions" on this point which will quite certainly have to be revised before long. It has been their favourite doctrine that most of the Pentateuch, instead of dating from Moses, comes down to us from the time of the Babylonian captivity, i.e., is not much older than 500 B.C. Yet the Samaritans, whose traditions are certainly pre-Exilic, hold the Pentateuch in no less reverence than their Jewish rivals. In fact, we have to suppose that the forgers who produced the Pentateuch, not only palmed off their fraud upon the Jewish public, but actually secured recognition for it from the intensely hostile and intensely conservative population of Samaria. A layman may be pardoned for feeling that such criticism as this is pure mythology. But, in view of the uncertainties which are prevalent, I mean to give here some estimate of the Jewish religious standpoint as a whole, without distinguishing the various alleged strata in the deposit, or claiming for the whole any very remote antiquity.

It will be noticed that the Jews, actuated by what they considered to be a Divine revelation, seem to have taken precisely that view of the Divine Nature which is, we have hitherto argued, the most rational view of it; they thought of God as an almighty, a transcendent, and a personal God. Poetry, and especially the poetry of Nature, gravitates at all times towards pantheism; yet the Jewish writers, with the strongest possible appreciation of Nature, at least in her wilder moods, never failed to argue back from the phenomena which they saw to the creative Power which produced them. Heaven was God's throne, earth his footstool; the day and the night were his couriers; it was the voice of the Lord that made the hinds to bring forth young, and shook the cedars of Libanus; in the permanence of the everlasting hills, in the strength of Leviathan, in the lion roaring after his prey, or the birds nesting in the trees, Jewish poetry could read but one lesson, repeated almost to monotony—the greatness of the Power to which all these effects were due. Their Palestinian neighbours were heathens, who saw in the yearly process of sun, rain, harvest, and vintage the influence of occult spiritual influences; yet the Jews never lost the sense, bred in them by their desert training, of a God infinitely remote, yet active in every fortune of man's life and in every phase of his natural surroundings.

It has, indeed, been suggested by critical historians that the religion of the Jews was at first monolatry, i.e., the worship of a tribal god, specially concerned with the fortunes of his own people, and existing side by side with a number of other tribal gods, his rivals; that it only developed by gradual stages into monotheism, i.e., belief in one God as the only God, with the accompanying conviction that rival "gods" had no existence except in the imagination of their votaries. Of any such development there is little proof, except what can be derived from an ad hoc manipulation of the evidence. What does seem clear is that there was, at all times, a popular tendency to lose sight of God's uniqueness, and to accord him merely an honoured place amidst a heathen Pantheon; but that this popular tendency was at all times counteracted by a noble series of patriots, reformers, and prophets, under whose influence the religious instinct of Judaism was constantly reverting to type. The notion that monotheism was a private discovery of the prophet Amos in something like 800 B.C. will hardly commend itself to the impartial observer who considers the intense obstinacy of the Jewish race, and its eager retentiveness of tradition.

As a condition of monotheism, the Jewish people had to be particularly on its guard against local worship, and against pictorial representations of the Divine Influence. Rival local cults of the same God will breed, in time, a multiplicity of Gods; dissimilar representations of the same God will be rationalised, in time, into different conceptions of God, and so into the conception of different gods. The Protestant division of the Decalogue, which distinguishes the prohibition of polytheism from the prohibition of idolatry as two separate commandments, is curiously untrue to the science (if it be a science) of comparative religion. Idolatry is at once the expression and the breeding-ground of polytheism. Here again, if our documents are worth anything at all, the history of the Jewish people is not the history of a development away from idolatry towards a more spiritual form of worship. It is the history of a series of alternations and struggles; the baser popular instinct of the Jews always hankering after visible gods and local sanctuaries, their religious leaders rallying them continually (always by an appeal to antiquity) and bringing them round again to the worship of that unique Spirit, whom the Heaven of heavens cannot contain.

Draw, for a moment, an imaginary line across the story of the past; forget all that has happened since the year 4 B.C.; rule out from your mind all the reverence with which centuries of Christianity have invested the Old Testament, all the prejudices which the accidents of later times have raised against the Jewish character as a factor in world history. Isolate in your mind the picture of a little people, assailed and half-infected by all the superstitions of the ancient world—the animal-worship of Egypt, the vegetation cults of the Canaanitish aborigines, the astrology of Babylon, the cultured anthropomorphism of classical Greece—yet ever obstinately retaining, after a thousand half-surrenders and tentative apostasies, the conception of a single God, unique in his majesty, controlling the destinies of all nations and all the forces of the created universe. Is there not, in that picture, something infinitely noble, some quality of unexpectedness which almost demands a special Divine revelation to account for it? Is it mere coincidence that amidst all the clash of Empires around the eastern shores of the Mediterranean, unchanged by the influence of Egyptian, Hittite, Assyrian, Syrian, Chaldean, or Phoenician civilisation, unconquered in its inmost hopes by the conquests of a Cyrus, an Alexander, or a Pompey, one tiny mountain people should have cherished like a sacred fire, its inviolable tradition of worship, should have upheld, to the unseeing eyes of pagan antiquity, a conception of fundamental theology which centuries of subsequent reflection have neither modified nor improved?

It is a spectacle which already provokes us to thought; makes us wonder whether God himself had not already, by means of some partial revelation, interfered to assist men's frantic guesses at his secret, and point their minds towards the truth. But it must be admitted that this distinctive tradition of worship is found side by side with a distinctive sense of nationality; religion and politics went hand in hand. The Jew was not more convinced of God's uniqueness than of the unique position which belonged to his own race. "They shall be my people, and I will be their God"; no cult of a tribal fetish was ever more conscientiously national. God is the King over all the earth; yet it has pleased him to select one only out of all the nations of the earth; one people whom he will honour with singular privileges, and visit with singular chastisements, because they are *his* people in a unique sense. Theirs is a covenanted position; fidelity is demanded on both sides—from them, to their national traditions, from God, to his promises of deliverance when deliverance is needed. The

effect of this bilateral contract is a curious one; it engages
Almighty God, who is *ex hypothesi* the Father of all mankind,
to concern himself with the fortunes of one particular race, to
the exclusion, apparently, of all other races under heaven. The
most inclusive of theologies is paradoxically maintained by
the most exclusive of peoples.

A monotheistic religion is commonly a missionary religion. It has no patience with the polytheism of its neighbours;
it cannot, like monolatry, apply a live-and-let-live principle to
the multiplicity of surrounding cults. To this principle Judaism forms a curious exception. Proselytes, indeed, existed as
an institution, and during the Captivity a notion seems to
emerge that the Dispersion of the Jews is intended by Providence to disseminate monotheism in the world (Tob 13:4).[1]
But, in general, Jewish thought seems to recognise a habitual
division of the world into the Jews and the godless Gentiles.
The key to this anomaly lay in the remote future. Some day
there would be a violent interference with the existing order
of things; there would be a triumphant vindication of God
and of his people; "a kingdom" would be set up which should
mirror on earth the perfect justice of heaven.

It is not only the Scriptural authors who assure us of this
attitude of expectancy; the extra-Biblical literature which is
known as "apocalyptic" or "eschatological" proves its popularity right down to the time of the Christian dispensation. It
looks as if the prophecy of Daniel, the most distinctively
apocalyptic of the Old Testament Scriptures, had produced a
crop of imitations, the Book of Enoch and all the rest of
them. These anticipations do not by any means agree in
matters of detail. Sometimes we hear, sometimes we do not

[1] "Because he hath therefore scattered you among the Gentiles, who know
not him, that you may declare his wonderful works: and make them know that
there is no other Almighty God beside him."

hear, of a personal Victor who is to usher in this kingdom; sometimes we might suppose him to be a man, sometimes he is clearly conceived as more than human—he is to come on the clouds of heaven; sometimes the Gentiles are to be crushed under the yoke of the conqueror, sometimes they are to live peaceably under his kingdom; sometimes a resurrection of the dead is to precede, sometimes it is to follow, the kingdom itself. But whatever the details, it seems clear that the Jews cherished a continual and a growing hope of final deliverance; that in the most disastrous times of their history, this hope did but grow the stronger; and that at the time of Christ's birth, at least among those faithful souls who "waited for the consolation of Israel", the fulfilment of all these prophecies was awaited with eager expectancy—perhaps through some mathematical calculations from the Book of Daniel, perhaps only because the events of the first century B.C. had given the death-blow to any idea of a merely political emancipation.

Thus the nation which had so curiously preserved, amidst a world of fantastic mythologies, a rational and a dignified conception of the Divine Nature was also unlike other nations in this—that it looked always to the future for the justification of its own existence. The Jew was proud of his national history, none more so; but he felt that the whole of this process was only the prelude to a mysterious "deliverance" in the future; a deliverance for which no political considerations gave him any ground for hope. The Jewish race walks backwards through history, its eyes turned towards the future, as one who heralds the coming of a king. It is as if the God whose Nature they had divined had determined to give the world a still fuller revelation of himself, and had chosen, first Abraham from his kindred, then Jacob from among his descendants, then Juda from among all the posterity of Jacob,

had preserved this people of his from so many perils of con-
quest, and had ransomed them from two captivities, only as
the preparation for some destiny hitherto unforeshadowed.

The moment at which John the Baptist's preaching found
so ready an echo in the hearts of his fellow-countrymen was
the worst possible moment for a successful Jewish insurrec-
tion. It would have had to encounter, not the undisciplined
armies of some Asiatic tyrant, but the grim, relentless pressure
of the Roman legions. On the other hand, it was the moment, humanly speaking, for a successful missionary cam-
paign in favour of some new propaganda. Within the last
three hundred years, the conquests of Alexander had spread,
up to the very gates of India, a uniform veneer of Greek
culture and familiarity with a common tongue. Within the
last hundred and fifty years, the conquests of the Roman arms
had, as if miraculously, brought the Mediterranean world into
the unity of a common political system. There had never
been more facility for travel and for the exchange of thought,
more freedom from hostile molestation. And through this
world of Greek speech and Greek culture, of Roman roads
and Roman institutions, the Jewish people, hitherto so stay-
at-home, so conservative, had pushed forward its outposts,
little colonies in Rome, in Alexandria, in Ephesus, in Corinth,
ready to act as centres for the propagation of a Jewish message.
Was it too much to say, in that age, that the fields were already
white to the harvest?

Let us add, at the risk of seeming fanciful, that something
of this atmosphere of expectancy which reigned among the
Jewish people had found its way into Gentile utterances, too.
After fifty years of continuous civil discord, even the urbane
Horace could feel the need of national regeneration, and sigh
for a Scythian caravan or a cruise to the Islands of the Blessed;
could ask what messenger Jupiter would send to expiate the

world's crimes; and Virgil, whatever the source of his inspiration, could break out into anticipations of a Golden Age which seem to reflect not only the thought but the language of Hebrew prophecy. These straws floating on the surface of polite literature indicate, surely, deeper currents of popular feeling underneath.

Such considerations as the foregoing will carry more weight with some minds than with others; I have only been at pains to write this crude frontispiece to the story of the Christian Revelation, because it does provide a sort of answer to a foolish but common objection which is sometimes raised against the truth of Christianity. Why should we be expected to pay so much attention (it is urged) to a particular set of events which happened at one particular moment of history in one particular corner of the ancient world? As if there was something provincial about the idea of God revealing himself at one time instead of another, in one place instead of another. Perhaps it will be a plaster for the irritation these scruples set up, to fall back upon the reflections I have here adduced—namely, that although Palestine was a small country and a provincial country, its religious history would, even apart from any Christian considerations, be something phenomenal among religious histories, and that the moment at which (we claim) the whole course of the world was changed was a moment which might well have been selected, or rather ordained, providentially, so full was it of conscious need and of practical opportunity. Nor need our religion be ashamed, in spite of modern sneers, of having taken root first in the seed-ground of Judaism. If the Christian religion could be proved an imposture, we should have to admit that, of all the great religions in the world, Judaism was the purest in its method of worship and the truest in its theological principles. A consideration which lends force to that pious Catholic belief, according to which Israel as a nation, before the last act closes on the world's drama, is to be convinced at last of its old blindness and brought into the fuller illumination of the Catholic Church.

VII

The Christian Evidences

In the last chapter, I invited my reader to put his hand across the page (so to speak) and leave out of sight all that has happened since the beginning of the Christian era; to treat the year 1 B.C. as if it were the limit of his historical knowledge. I will now ask him, if I may pursue the same metaphor, to take his hand away, all except the top finger—to blot out from memory all that he knows of what happened between 1 B.C. and A.D. 100, and to look with fresh eyes at the literature of the period which immediately follows the Twelve Cæsars; the literature, roughly speaking, that dates between A.D. 90 and 120.

You find the world still pagan; the same tradition of Greco-Roman culture persists, not menaced hitherto by grave corruption within, or formidable competition from without. Meanwhile, the Jewish race has disappeared from view, for the time being, as completely as it has ever disappeared in history. Jerusalem has been sacked, not one stone left on another; and with the loss of its nerve-centre the active life of Judaism seems temporarily suspended; the Roman satirist only connects it with the soothsayers, who practised upon the fashionable superstitions of the day.

At the same time, in Bithynia, a province very far distant from Judea, a Roman governor with great conscientiousness and some mildness of disposition, the younger Pliny, is becoming exercised over a pressing imperial problem. He writes to the Emperor Trajan to know if he has been right in the policy which he has adopted towards the troublesome sect of the Christians.

There is no reason to think that the difficulty was merely local; that Bithynia was more infested with Christians than other provinces in the Hellenised portion of the Roman world. We have no statistics, but it is evident that the criminals in question were sufficiently numerous; both Pliny and Trajan are anxious to discourage the activities of the informer (a sure sign that you are afraid of learning the true strength of your adversaries); and not a few, it would appear, of the accused renounced their opinions under the threat of punishment—the movement, therefore, was already sufficiently fashionable to be attracting half-hearted supporters. Pliny has heard various tales to the discredit of these strange votaries, tales of incestuous marriages and of child-eating; but he confesses that in all his inquiries he has found no evidence to support such charges. On the contrary, it appears that the Christians are bound by an oath or sacrament to abstain from all crime against their neighbours, and their secret meetings involve nothing more serious than a religious service which includes a sacramental meal, and the singing of a hymn "to Christ as God". Those who consent to offer sacrifice to the emblems of the heathen deities and of the Emperor himself are dismissed with a caution; those who remain obstinate are ordered, by a convenient euphemism, to be "led away".

This need for repressive action against the Christians—breaking the butterfly sect upon the wheel of imperial efficiency—had been felt, though perhaps dimly felt, much earlier.

A historian, Tacitus, Pliny's contemporary and friend, describes how Nero, fifty years before, had sent Roman Christians to the stake. Tacitus is an unfriendly witness, and describes the Christians as "hated on account of their crimes"; but then, so doubtless would Pliny until he acquired first-hand experience in Bithynia. In a great city like Rome one does not know one's neighbours; and the most fantastic reports gain easy credit when they are circulated against a religion which is practised in secret. No hint of revolutionary or unpatriotic action on the Christians' part is ever dropped, unless it be in the statement of Suetonius that the Jews were banished from Rome because they were "making continual disturbances under the instigation of Christus", which may conceivably have reference to differences between Christians and Jews.

That the founder of this sect suffered under Tiberius, we have Tacitus' evidence; for a fuller account of his character we might go to the Jewish historian Josephus, who, writing a little earlier, gives a thumb-nail sketch of the career of one Jesus of Nazareth, whom he identifies with Christus in a footnote. But the suspicion of Christian additions to the text forbids us to accept without hesitation the further details of this remarkable passage. There is no reason whatever to suspect the allusions in Tacitus of being later, Christian interpolations; there is a complete absence of external proof, and the references themselves proclaim their genuineness by their moderation; a Christian interpolator would assuredly have made a better job of it.

So much we should know (I am giving only the more salient instances, and the outlines of them, not the details) even if Christian literature had wholly disappeared from the face of the planet. We should know that between the years 60 and 120 the Jewish people had lost the limited political importance which it had hitherto enjoyed, and that, during the same years, a sect which originated on Jewish soil (but was certainly quite unconnected with official Judaism) had spread across Asia Minor to the coasts of the Black Sea, and across Greece to the imperial capital itself; that in spite of rigid persecution its determined opposition to idolatry, and therefore to Cæsar-worship, had become an imperial problem which needed constant reference to headquarters; and that a central part of its creed was the Divinity of Christus, a Man who suffered under Tiberius somewhere about A.D. 30. The record would surely strike us as a curious one. No public action had had to be taken, as far as we know, against any religion as such, since the (purely local) suppression of the Bacchanals at Rome early in the second century B.C. That there were other secret religions which enjoyed some popularity during the first century we are well aware. Orphic mysteries and Isis-worship and so on. No doubt Christianity resembled them, as it resembles many other religions, in having its secret pass-words, its ceremony of initiation, its sacramental meal; it may even have adopted into its language some of their jargon about initiation, illumination, and the rest. But the most fantastic speculations have failed to prove any trace of interconnection; and meanwhile it is obviously unscientific to classify Christianity among the mystery cults. For Christianity has salient qualities which utterly distinguish it from them. The mystery religions not only contrived to live on terms with the old heathen worship, but actually busied themselves in tracing their origin to one or other of the well-known figures in classical mythology. Christianity, from the first moment of its appearance, dates its origin quite frankly from the year A.D. 30, and regards all the figures of heathen mythology as abominations. Consequently Christianity, unlike the mystery religions, was persecuted in the name of pagan theology, and its tenets were supposed to be incompatible with the duties of a good citizen. As a mere matter of observation, Christianity is from the first *sui generis*, and Judaism is the only system which approaches in any way to its strangely exclusive and intolerant attitude.

Let us now turn our attention to the documents of the same period (A.D. 90–120) which come to us from Christian sources—the Epistles, let us say, of Ignatius and Clement. Here you find the record of an institutional religion already firmly established, with a definite creed and a definite system of Church government. You find abundant material to corroborate Pliny's statement that the Christians worshipped Christ as God; you find the explanation of this attitude in the conviction that Christ rose from the dead. You find a marked antagonism towards the whole genius of paganism, and a firm belief that death suffered in defiance of heathenism is the preface to a glorious immortality. You find a habit of epistolography—the individual addressing his message to an assembled "church"—which assumes the existence of an established model (a Pauline model, as we shall see later). You find the clear confidence that the whole of Judaism was only a preparation for Christianity. You find the assumption that Christianity is everywhere represented by a common type, with an overseer (or "bishop") in control. You find that the centre of all this system is already fixed at the metropolitan city of Rome; since Clement, in the name of the Church there, addresses his expostulations to fellow-Christians on the other side of the Adriatic who had revolted against their "priests", and Ignatius credits the same Church with an imperfectly defined title to presidency. So much for Christianity in the second generation, an impressive proof of its uncompromising attitude and its rapid development, even if no earlier documents were available. But, as we know, we have a set of documents in our possession, most of which are certainly anterior in date to the period we have been considering—I mean the documents which go to form the New Testament Scriptures. I need hardly remind the reader that in this and the next three chapters those documents will be treated, not as if they had any claim upon our faith as authoritative formulas of religion, but merely as historical documents whose value must be estimated according to historical principles.

We have a series of "epistles", some of them genuine letters, written to satisfy an immediate demand, some of them treatises in epistolary form. A round dozen of these come from the same hand; the incoherency of their style, the embarrassed egotism of the author's attitude, his insistent and sometimes irrelevant reiteration of a few favourite doctrinal principles, are the hall-mark of their unity. Nor is there any serious doubt, on internal or external grounds, that they are what they profess to be—the work of Paul, a propagandist of the new religion who had been particularly active in European Greece and on the sea-board of Asia Minor. His principal preoccupations in writing seem to have been (1) to define the exact relations, at that time sufficiently obscure, between Christianity and its foster-parent Judaism; (2) to collect money for the needs of the poor Christians at Jerusalem; (3) to assert his own accredited position as a Christian missionary, in answer to various critics who tried to represent him as a free-lance. But he also deals individually with local problems; as, the exaggerated enthusiasm of Corinth, the premature fears of a world-upheaval felt in Macedonia, and the danger of contamination from superstitious cults at Ephesus and Colossæ.

These letters, from internal evidence or from comparison with another document to be mentioned presently, have to be dated earlier, for the most part, than A.D. 60. In reading them, the unbiased critic can hardly fail to be struck by the following points:

1. That in spite of the confusion introduced by the competition of rival missionaries, it is constantly assumed that the Christians of the world form a single body. The local "church" is only the model of a potentially world-wide institution, *the* Church.

2. That this Church consists of those who have made an act of faith in Christ, which is identified in significance with the outward ceremony of baptism.

3. That the Christian Church, young as it is, has already traditions which are to be maintained, and a fixed deposit of belief.

4. That faith in Christ implies assent to the doctrine that he rose from the dead, a fact attested by various witnesses, of whom, in virtue of a particular moment of mystical experience, Paul considers himself one.

5. That Christ is, in a few texts, explicitly identified as God; and that the general place assigned to him in the scheme of "Redemption" is inconsistent with the supposition that his dignity is other than Divine.

6. That the covenant under which the Jewish Church claimed to be the chosen Assembly of God has now been superseded by a fresh covenant with an international Assembly, the Christian Church.

7. That idolatry, or even co-operation in idolatry, is directly contrary to the Christian profession; Christians have a sacrificial meal or ceremony of their own, the supernatural character of which is elsewhere explicitly asserted.

Side by side with these epistles goes a book which even the more rigorous critics attribute to a companion of Paul, and date before A.D. 70 or very soon after it, the Acts of the Apostles. The first part of this book gives a historical sketch of this Christian Church in its earliest beginnings, of which the whole tone is obviously primitive; the second part contains an account of Paul's missionary activities, and shows for the most part the work of an eye-witness. This document entirely bears out the account of Christianity which we have already derived from Paul's epistles, and adds something to the definiteness of the picture; e.g., it describes assemblies of leading Christians which clearly regard themselves as empowered to legislate for the welfare of the Church, and it records the ceremonial imposition of hands, both upon the newly baptised and upon men singled out to take part in the work of evangelisation. We need not consider the other "epistles", of non-Pauline or doubtfully Pauline origin, since they do not add much to the picture for our present purposes.

Suppose that were all. Suppose, *par impossible*, that we had no Gospels. What would be, and what ought to be our attitude towards the Catholic Church? We should at least have to admit that this extraordinary institution has persisted for nearly nineteen hundred years, accused, sometimes, of over-definition, but never of cancelling its beliefs, of development, but never of any break in its historic continuity. We should have to admit that its career is highly documented back to the very date of its Founder's death, or at worst to within twenty years of it; that its main structure, the more intimate of its doctrines and the more prominent of its ceremonies, had remained unaltered through the centuries. That its chief credential, from the first, had been this amazing story of a dead Man coming to life; and that it had imposed this belief, in the first instance, on people who were that Man's contemporaries, and had been living in the very country, in the very city, where his death took place. That it had absorbed into itself, before long, the energies of that religious movement which John the Baptist had initiated; that it had claimed to fulfil the age-long expectation of the Jewish people at the moment when its fulfilment was expected. We should have had to admit that it was worth while questioning an institution like this, and finding out what story it had to tell.

And it would have told us its story, handed down by word of mouth through the centuries, and verifiable only by stray allusions, here and there, in the literature of those centuries. How its own Founder was miraculously born, in fulfilment of Isaias' prophecy; how John bore witness to him; how he fasted and was tempted in the desert; how he went about doing good, and how he taught, and, how his teaching roused against him the envious spite of the Jewish leaders; how he performed miracles, fed five thousand men with five loaves, and walked on the sea, and raised the dead, even, to life; the circumstances of his betrayal, judgment, and death. All this would have been enshrined in the oral traditions of the Church, as it must have been in the days before the Gospels were written—those first converts, surely, asked questions? And the apostles who had lived with the Christ had some answers, surely, to satisfy their curiosity? We should have been in the same position; only that an occasional literary allusion could have been quoted, here and there, in support of the traditional statement.

We are not left to depend on an oral tradition. For the tradition itself was written down, before the scent (you may say) had had time to grow cold, by four separate chroniclers. The story they tell is a curiously incomplete one, if you judge it by the principles of modern biography. It is only a fragment, but it has left an ineffaceable picture upon the imagination of mankind. It takes back the oral tradition, not indeed to the very earliest times of Christianity, but to a period so little removed from them that there is little fear of its misrepresenting apostolic belief. Three of these chronicles, at least, must have been written when men still lived who had had speech with the Christ, and could check the facts recorded. It is to this documentary tradition, then, that we go for our picture of Christ's Life. Indeed, for practical purposes it is all we have left to us. For the documentary tradition replaces, and so kills, the oral tradition. It is extraordinary how few legends there are, with any respectable claim to authenticity, to supplement the Gospel story. It is extraordinary how few sayings of our Lord have been preserved (there is one in Acts 20:35) [1] which are not recorded in the Gospels themselves. Men will not trust their memory when they have written sources to refer to.

The text of these four documents is as well established as any text could be. Owing to their frequent transcription, the manuscripts must have divided very early into different "families", and it is unlikely that the text of any one "family" should have become extinct. This division into families has left its traces, naturally, on the manuscripts we still possess, but none of the differences is sufficiently serious to concern our present purpose. The text of the Gospel record can be taken as a fixed quantity; and it is only by risking all their reputation as textual critics that scholars can have the hardihood to question the genuineness of a single verse (as some have questioned Matthew 28:19), so strong is the consensus of manuscript evidence.

There is far less general agreement as to the authorship of the Gospels and the written sources, if any, which lie behind them. A mass of ponderous learning has been accumulating, these hundred years past, over the "Synoptic problem", and

[1] ". . . remember the word of the Lord Jesus, how he said: It is a more blessed thing to give than to receive."

we are no nearer the solution of it. The fact is that in our day we have no real qualifications for pronouncing on "documentary hypotheses"; for deciding whether document A was copied from document B, or vice versa, or whether both were copied from a lost source C; whether, in that case, C was another document or an oral tradition; how much revision and "editing" is to be expected from the men who finally put the documents into shape. Infinite ingenuity has been bestowed upon the task, but we lack experience. Printing has made everything so easy for us that we have no longer any means of judging what was probable or improbable in the first century, what were the chances of a document getting lost, getting mutilated, getting surreptitiously altered; how much authors worked by memory, how much by consulting their authorities; how much they allowed their order of arrangement to be interfered with by considerations of practical convenience. I propose, then, in the following chapter to treat the Synoptic record as a promiscuous whole. It is enough for us to notice that the wilder extravagances of criticism are now obsolescent, and that we can, without attracting the derision of scholars, treat the first three Gospels as documents dating back behind A.D. 70—that is, documents written within the lifetime of people who were grown up when the events in question took place.

The Fourth Gospel—I must repeat, we are not here treating the Bible as an inspired record—we must use more charily. If we accept the tradition of its authorship, it seems probable that it was the work of a man in extreme old age, and the objector might legitimately question whether his memory was still accurate. Many modern scholars refuse to accept the tradition, and would put the record outside the first century altogether. From its very nature it is a baffling subject of study. People will tell you that it is, for the most part, a work of philosophic reflection, casting Christian doctrine, by a dramatic device, into monologue or dialogue form. For myself, I confess that it reads to me much more like the laborious recollections of a very old man, meticulously accurate about unimportant details, merely in order to show that he does remember them, and constantly forgetting what stage he has reached (as old men will) in the story or in the argument. But, whatever be said of it, it seems clear at least that in some of its main outlines it preserves an independent tradition. The very fact that it corrects the ideas we might otherwise have formed about the length of our Lord's ministry, the day of his Passion, etc., is good proof that it does not depend entirely on the other Gospels for its representation of the incidents. This fourth record, then, must also be taken into account if we are to form a complete view of the evidence at our disposal.

In order to confine our considerations as far as possible to matters of practical importance, I shall make no attempt to recall to the reader the details of a Life so familiar as that of our Lord. I shall pursue, in the two following chapters, two isolated lines of argument; asking first whether the Founder of Christianity did himself claim to be God, and then, granting that he did, how far his claim can be justified by a study of his Personality and of his career.

VIII

Our Lord's Claim Stated

The statement that our Lord claimed to be God has to be qualified in two respects. In the first place, he did not "claim" to be God in the sense of loudly asserting such a claim, of insisting on it in season and out of season. On the contrary, he was at pains, during most of his life, to silence speculation on the subject. Which is the best possible proof that in his own Mind he believed himself to be God. You do not silence speculation, unless it is in danger of arriving at the truth; you do not silence speculation, when you could dispose of it more easily by a denial. In the second place, our Lord did not claim to be God only; he claimed, also, to be Man. At certain times in his Life he seems to have insisted strongly on the reality of his human nature. And this, again, is the best possible proof that he believed himself to be God; he would not have paraded his Humanity if he had not felt there was some danger that his Humanity would be overlooked or forgotten. Let us begin by enlarging a little on these two points.

Some critics of the Gospels have written as though our Lord's consciousness of his "Messiahship" was a notion which dawned upon him gradually and strengthened as his Life proceeded. This is a pure speculation, which sins by going

beyond the evidence. The evidence is not that the consciousness dawned gradually upon him, but that he allowed it to
dawn gradually on the rest of the world. The fact that he
forbade the "devils" to call him Christ early in his ministry,
yet encouraged Peter to call him Christ later in his ministry,
does not define the limit of what he knew, but of what he
wished to be known. And there can be little doubt in any
candid mind which reads the four records merely as records
that his self-revelation was a gradual revelation. It was natural,
if not necessary, that it should be. The Jews, it is clear, were
not expecting a Messiah who should come amongst them as
a man amongst men; they looked for a Deliverer from the
clouds. Their ideas, therefore, had to be gradually remod-
elled. Their minds had to be accustomed gradually to the idea
that this was something more than Man.

Hence, from the first, he refused the tribute of recognition
offered him by the demoniacs; when they hailed him as the
Son of God, he bade them hold their peace. Even to his own
most intimate friends he did not betray his secret at first. At
various times his apostles seem to have had an inkling of the
truth (Matthew 14:33,[1] John 1:49[2]). Yet it is clear that the
Synoptic Gospels regard St. Peter's Confession as the first
formal expression of a fully-rooted conviction on the subject.
It was a conviction (according to these Evangelists) only
gradually produced on their minds by a series of miracles
(Mark 6:52),[3] and produced with a slowness which occasioned surprise to their Master himself (Mark 8:21).[4] Even

[1] "And they that were in the boat came and adored him, saying: Indeed thou
art the Son of God."

[2] "Nathaniel answered him and said: Rabbi: Thou art the Son of God. Thou
art the King of Israel."

[3] "For they understood not concerning the loaves: for their heart was
blinded."

[4] "And he said to them: How do you not yet understand?"

after Peter's Confession, the great secret must be kept within the apostolic circle (Mark 8:30);[5] and it has been plausibly conjectured, though without any certain evidence, that part of Judas' treachery lay in his being prepared to divulge the secret. The Jews at large must not be told it; they must be left to find it out for themselves, and react upon it as they would (Mark 4:11).[6] Even John, whose record seems to represent our Lord as comparatively outspoken in his teaching about himself, bears witness that the Jews were uncertain, almost to the last, as to whether he claimed to be Christ or no (John 8:25,[7] 10:24[8]). A premature assertion of his own claim would, it seems certain, have led to a crown in Galilee, a shower of stones in Judea. The nation, then, must be left to learn its own lesson. As they listened to our Lord's teaching, as they listened, in particular, to the oracular sense conveyed by his parables, the Pharisees were constantly hoping to find a frank avowal of what they considered blasphemous pretensions; they were not successful till the very eve of the Passion, when the parable of the Wicked Husbandmen lifted at last the veil of conscious Divinity (Mark 12:12).[9]

Our Lord's claim to Godhead was, therefore, a claim present to his own Mind, not one which he flourished before the world. On the contrary, he was at pains to obscure it from the world; and that policy of obscuration is good evidence, for any who will consider its meaning, of what his

[5] "And he strictly charged them that they should not tell any man of him."

[6] "And he said to them: To you it is given to know the mystery of the kingdom of God: but to them that are without, all things are done in parables."

[7] "They therefore said to him: Who art thou? Jesus said to them: The beginning, who also speak unto you."

[8] "The Jews therefore came round about him and said to him: How long dost thou hold our souls in suspense? If thou be the Christ tell us plainly."

[9] "And they sought to lay hands on him: but they feared the people. For they knew that he spoke this parable to them. And leaving him they went their way."

inward convictions were. On two occasions, at least, our Lord seems to have gone to the opposite extreme, and deliberately asserted the fact of his Humanity, as if apprehensive lest after his death his followers should forget he had ever been human. The story of his Temptation (we are not arguing here its historical value) is a story which in the nature of the case can only have been told by himself. Why did he go out of his way to tell it, unless he was determined to prove that he could suffer, as Man, the exterior assaults of temptation; and that he would meet those assaults simply as Man, refusing to gratify the curiosity of his Enemy as to whether he were more than Man (Matthew 4:6)? And his Agony in the garden of Gethsemani shows once more the intention to parade (you might almost say) his human weakness. He insisted upon having witnesses at hand precisely when any of us who had the normal instincts of courage would have wished to be alone—when he knew that he was going to "break down". I have never been able to make any sense of these two stories, except on the assumption that our Lord meant to say, "See, I am Man, although I am God"—and in issuing that caution, it is clear that, *ex hypothesi*, he admits the fact of his own Divinity.

In a word, the arguments which are most commonly urged against our Lord's Divine claim—his silence about it, his insistence on the fact of his Humanity—are, properly viewed, indirect evidences in the opposite sense. So, for that matter, is the well-known rejoinder, "Why dost thou call me good? None is good, save God"—a rejoinder which is exquisitely flat and meaningless if it be taken as a serious statement, full of significance when you realise that it was uttered in irony. But now, cannot these indirect evidences be supplemented by direct evidences, by any positive statement on our Lord's own part?

The position which our Lord's language actually claims is one which can only be inferred from a variety of considerations. (1) In the first place, he definitely identifies himself with the "Son of Man" who is to come in judgment either at the beginning or at the end of the Messianic kingdom. It is quite certain that our Lord referred to himself as the Son of Man (e.g., Luke 9:58).[10] It is equally certain that he looked forward to the return of the Son of Man in judgment (e.g., Matthew 25:31).[11] There is no question that Daniel, and the eschatological writings in imitation of Daniel, had described the Inaugurator of the new world-order as the Son of Man (Daniel 7:14).[12] It is probable indeed, that this title was deliberately chosen as being a non-committal title; it was (in the modern phrase) "not actionable". But it was a title to set men wondering whether he who used it did not claim to be the fulfilment of Israel's hopes, and the Arbiter of its destiny.

(2) Our Lord constantly referred to himself *by implication* as the Son of God. To prove this, it is not necessary to have recourse to various texts in St. John, disallowed by the moderns. It is sufficient to observe that when he teaches his disciples to pray, he begins his model petition with the words "our Father". Nowhere else in his teaching do the words "our Father" occur. Constantly he speaks to his disciples of "my Father who is in heaven", constantly of "your Father who is in heaven", but never of "our Father who is in heaven". Could any clearer proof be needed that he thought of himself as the Son of God in a peculiar sense, in which that title could not be shared with any merely human creature, even with the

---

[10] "Jesus said to him: The foxes have holes, and the birds of the air nests; but the Son of Man hath not where to lay his head."

[11] "And when the Son of Man shall come in his majesty, and all the angels with him, then shall he sit upon the seat of his majesty."

[12] ". . . And lo, one like the son of man came with the clouds of heaven . . ."

apostles themselves? The intimate relation which exists between the Son and the Father is attested, not only by the
evidence of St. John, but by that of St. Matthew (11:27)[13] and
St. Luke (10:22).

(3) In all the descriptions of our Lord's miracles—I am not
at present concerned to defend their miraculous character,
but they form an integral part of the record—there is no
suggestion that he intends to exercise miraculous powers in
any other Name than his own. It must be remembered that,
to Jewish minds, "who only doeth great wonders" was a
characteristic description of Almighty God. The miracles of
the Old Testament, like the miracles of ecclesiastical history,
were normally due, it appears, to an invocation of the Divine
Power; our Lord never invokes the Divine Power. Sometimes, indeed, his intervals of silence suggest that he is en-
gaging in mental prayer. But the actual word which heals or
commands is his own *ipse dixit*—a significant fact, when we
remember the intensely jealous monotheism of the Jewish
people. It may be added that our Lord never discourages a
posture of worship in those who address him (e.g., Matthew
9:18).[14]

It remains true, however, that our Lord made no statement,
at least in public, which could be represented as claiming
Divine honours for himself; otherwise, assuredly, his enemies
would have had no difficulty in finding material for his condemnation. It appears that the most definite charge which
was brought against him was that of having said, "Destroy this
temple, and in three days I will raise it up." It is unlikely that

[13] "All things are delivered to me by my Father. And no one knoweth the
Son, but the Father: neither doth anyone know the Father, but the Son and he
to whom it shall please the Son to reveal *him*."

[14] "As he was speaking these things unto them, behold a certain ruler came
and adored him, saying: Lord, my daughter is even now dead; but come, lay thy
hand upon her and she shall live."

our Lord was accused of disrespect towards the Temple; there is no evidence that any such charge figured in the prosecution. It must rather be supposed that the assumption of independence which the words indicated was understood to imply powers more than human. But even this accusation was inconclusive; it remained only for the High Priest to put the direct question, Art thou the Christ, the Son of the Blessed God? To which the answer is given "I am. Nevertheless I say to you, Hereafter you shall see the Son of Man sitting on the right hand of the power of God, and coming with the clouds of heaven" (Mark 14:62, Matthew 26:64).

What is the sense of the High Priest's question? For the answer to it must surely be judged according to the sense of the interrogator. It was not the time for ambiguous replies, which might have distorted the course of justice. Our Lord answered what Caiphas asked, and in the sense in which Caiphas questioned him. It is clear, in the first place, that our Lord meant to identify himself with the Messiah, that mysterious Figure who was to usher in the age of Israel's deliverance. This Messiah was expected to come to earth in visible glory with his angels in attendance; will the Galilean claim to have fulfilled *that* prophecy? To which our Lord answers, "I am the Christ, and *it is not now but hereafter* that you will see the Christ sitting on the right hand of the power of his Father, and coming in the clouds of heaven." (This is clearly the sense of the "hereafter" preserved by Matthew, who in this passage at least, *pace* the critics, has the original account.) But, so multitudinous were the prophecies understood to refer to the Messiah, it was not quite clear that "the Christ" was necessarily a Divine title. Caiphas gives it further precision by adding "the Son of the Blessed God".

Is it possible to suppose that the words "Son of God" used in such a connection could be applicable to a peculiarly exalted representative of the human race, or even to some angelic being? Not if we may trust St. John, who usually shows himself an accurate reporter of Jewish customs; a comparison between verses 33 and 36 of John 10 proves that in his mind, at least, the titles "God" and "Son of God" were identical. Nor according to the probabilities of Jewish thought: the notion of demigods or heroes might be familiar to the pagan world, with its half-pantheistic conceptions of divinity; but the Jew had so strong a sense of the absolute difference, the unbridged gulf, between God and man, that it is hard to suppose any created Being could be described as the Son of God in a unique sense. Nor, again, in virtue of what followed; is it possible that the unanimous cry of "Blasphemy!" should have greeted our Lord's utterance, if it were possible to explain away that utterance as merely laying claim to some kind of angelic existence? You might almost say that, whatever significance Jewish thought attached, before then, to the word *Messiah*, this decision of the Council constituted it a Divine title thenceforward.

The force of the foregoing arguments is perhaps best realised if the reader will put to himself the following question: "If Jesus of Nazareth did not claim to be God, what *did* he claim to be?" Is it credible that he did what he did, said what he said, hinted what he hinted, kept silence where he kept silence, and finally answered the challenge of Caiphas without a word of qualification, of explanation, or of self-defence, if all the time he belonged, and was conscious of belonging, to any order of Being less than Divine? Where was the need of all this mystery, these veiled allusions, these injunctions of silence, if they only served to foster a false impression which a couple of sentences would have cleared up? And finally, how could language such as that of Paul in Philippians 2:6 pass unrebuked, unless the Christians of Paul's time, like the Christians of Pliny's time, were accustomed to address their devotions to Christ as God?

I do not mean to suggest that it is necessary for the apologist, at this stage in the proceedings, to establish the fact of our Lord's Divinity as such. All our argument demands is the proof that he came with the avowed intention of communicating a Divine revelation, and the further proof that a power manifestly Divine set its seal unmistakably upon this claim of his—that he was an accredited ambassador from God to men. If the arguments hitherto adduced are justified, it is clear that he who claimed to be God did, a fortiori, claim to announce an authoritative revelation. If we can only establish that, it will follow that the movement which he inaugurated, the Church which he founded, is of Divine institution, and that whatever promises he has made to it carry with them that absolute guarantee which is based on the Divine Fidelity. Had he definitely restricted his claim to an authority less than absolute, we might have reverenced him as a voice sent from God, yet suspected that, through human weakness, some of his promises were exaggerated. If he took rank as a Man, as the greatest of the world's mystics, his revelations would have been open to the same doubt as the revelations of the mystics themselves. But, if he claimed full authority, shall we not believe that the purpose of his coming was providentially secured from miscarriage, and that the Church, as the sole visible legacy he left behind him, was providentially equipped for bringing that purpose to its fulfilment?

IX

Our Lord's Claim Justified

It belongs to the courtesies of duelling that the challenger should offer his opponent a choice of weapons. In this debate, which here reaches its critical point, it is the Catholic Church which challenges the human intellect. In courtesy, therefore, the reader must be allowed his choice of weapons, if he is prepared to abide by it.

If you are prepared to admit the possibility of miracle, then you will naturally expect that an event so full of importance for the human race as a personal revelation from Almighty God should be accompanied by evidences of his miraculous power. It will be my object in the later part of this chapter to show that the Christian revelation fulfils the conditions so laid down. But if you are determined, from some preconceived prejudice, some strange inhibition of thought, to rule out the possibility of miracle; if you are prepared to dismiss as a fiction any story which involves a miracle, for the reason that it involves a miracle and for no other—then I will do my best to give you satisfaction on your own terms; but you must abide by your own terms. You must consider, in all honesty, whether the life of our Lord does not give you every possible assurance of his Divinity, short of a miracle. I do not say that such assurance would ever satisfy me, but it must satisfy you. It must satisfy you, because it is precisely the kind of assurance you have demanded. You must not say that no revelation would satisfy you unless the guarantee of miracle accompanied it, and then say in the same breath that you will refuse to accept any story of miracle precisely on the ground that it is miraculous. That is as if you were to invite your opponent to stab you with a pistol. If you will not have miracles, then you must be prepared to be satisfied without them.

Let us then, for the time being, and for the sake of argument, dismiss from our minds the whole notion of the miraculous. Let us suppose that the healing powers which our Lord exercised did not go beyond faith-healing; that the Empty Tomb was an illusion, the Resurrection a mere survival of the Spirit, the Resurrection appearances a series of visions. What judgment shall we then pass on the career of Jesus of Nazareth, this Man who claimed to be God?

If our Lord was not God, yet claimed to be God, he must either have been a conscious Impostor, or else the Victim of a hallucination. It is not easy for a Christian to discuss either alternative with patience; fortunately, the first does not call for much discussion. It is bad criticism to explain a career on a theory of conduct for which no motive can be assigned. It is quite evident that our Lord had no political ambitions, for he constantly refused, in spite of obvious precedents, in spite of eager encouragement, to appear in a political *rôle*. Nor can it have been his aim to amass money; for he lived and died a poor Man, and did so, clearly, of his own choice. Nor was he one of those who take delight in the plaudits of the crowd; he constantly withdrew himself from the crowd, and took refuge beyond Jordan, precisely where he would not be recognised, and where, indeed, his popularity was limited

(Mark 5:17).[1] Nor, apart from the question of motive, does it seem possible that a deliberate effort to deceive his contemporaries should be consistent with all that we know about Jesus of Nazareth, his humility, his love of retirement, his hatred of shams and hypocrisies.

Yet, if this plea is disallowed, it seems that we have to fall back on a plea equally distasteful—on the suggestion, not unknown in his own day, that he was mad. Not, indeed, that this plea can be ruled out of court with a wave of the hand. The history of enthusiasm bears painful witness that it is possible for a man to show marks of great spirituality, and to become the founder of a religious movement, although loss of reason is the only charitable account we can give of his total attitude. It would be absurd to deny that an intense and apparently sincere preoccupation with religion does sometimes unsettle a man's wits. You cannot argue, in so many words, that So-and-so is too good a man to be suspected of delusions. The charge, however distasteful to pious ears, must be dealt with on its merits.

The real refutation of it seems to me to lie in this—that the suggestion of madness is inconsistent with the breadth of vision and the originality of thought (to put it at its lowest) which are displayed by our Lord's teaching. In madness there may be glimpses of inspiration; nobody who has read Christopher Smart's "Hymn to David" can doubt that it was the work of a madman, or can help feeling that it would be almost worth going mad to be able to write like that. "Kubla Khan" was written under the influence of a drug, and I suppose there are a few other instances in which good work has been done under such abnormal conditions. But, on the average, that liberation of the unconscious which is secured by madness, by drug-taking, and by certain other influences

[1] "And they began to pray him that he would depart from their coasts."

is lamentably disappointing in its results. The letters of lunatics—how inexpressibly *boring* they are, to say nothing of their other qualities! The results obtained by automatic writing, or by spiritualistic mediumship, how signally they have failed to enrich the world's literature by a single new thought! If you take mere literary interest as a criterion, who, unless he were a devotee, has ever read with patience Swedenborg's "Heaven and Hell", or the "Book of Mormon"? But surely, if every vestige of the Christian religion should disappear from the planet, the words spoken by Jesus of Nazareth would still be read for their own beauty. Even in the mongrel Greek in which they have been preserved to us, they challenge attention. Agree with them or disagree with them, do they not provide *food for thought* beyond anything which the pale mystics of the East have ever achieved? Are they not, whatever they are, a permanent addition to the triumphs of the human genius?

Lunacy does not fail to give itself away. As well expect a motor-car to find its way through crowded traffic without a driver, as a mind that is unbalanced to commit itself to literary expression without being guilty of extravagances that betray it. Imagine, if you will, that the words attributed to our Lord in the Fourth Gospel really enshrine the ideas of a later Christian thinker, you cannot give the same account of the Synoptic teaching. For, in the first place, you have to give some account of the following which our Lord had during his lifetime; you have already disallowed his miracles—if you censor his teaching too, what cause will you have left to explain his popularity? And in the second place you have to account for the origin of these alleged sayings—what source will you assign to them? It is true, the manner of our Lord's teaching is Rabbinical, and some of his utterances have their parallels in Rabbinical literature; but is it conceivable that the whole corpus of his doctrine is a mere anthology from earlier sources? Why, then, was it not challenged? For the records on which we depend were published within forty years of his death; and, if the modern critics are to be trusted, these records are themselves dependent on a much earlier document. Did no one, in those earlier times, question its authenticity? The utterances attributed to Socrates may be of doubtful genuineness, but that is because we know that his biographer was a Plato. What Plato had our Lord to report him? No one who values his reputation as a critic will dispute that, whoever Jesus of Nazareth was, he was the author of the words attributed to Jesus of Nazareth in the first three Gospels. Those Gospels are, on the face of it, the work of commonplace biographers, who can hardly be suspected of scientific editing. How is it, then, that the words of Jesus Christ bear all the marks, not of religious mania, but of religious genius?

I say, then, that even if you disallow all miraculous evidence you have still to find your way out of an *impasse*. You have to commit yourself to one of the three following statements: (1) Jesus Christ did not claim to be God. (2) Jesus Christ was a conscious Impostor. (3) Jesus Christ was a religious Maniac. Which of these three theses will you select for defence, and on what ground will you defend it? To hazard the opinion that any one of these three contentions may be true, you cannot tell which, is to be guilty of the utmost intellectual laziness, a laziness which few honestly-minded men will hesitate to pronounce culpable.

For myself, leaving the sceptic to these embarrassments, I do not hesitate to say that I find this argument, whatever its logical cogency, more satisfactory as a contribution to proof than as a proof in itself. I do not believe that, human nature being what it is, the immediate impression made by the preaching of the Gospel could have been so profound, if its first missionaries had only told to the world the story of a Man, clearly not mad, clearly not an Impostor, who was nevertheless prepared to accept the worship due to a God. And indeed, if it is permissible for us to lay down any a priori principles by which we should have expected a Revelation to be regulated, it is surely clear that we should have expected something more than this. God is revealed to us in his works, as we saw, in three ways. The witness of our conscience directs us to him as All-Righteous; the consideration of the order which reigns in Nature directs us to him as All-Wise; and the mere fact of Creation itself, with the forces which control its conditions, directs us to him as All-Powerful. Surely an adequate revelation should satisfy the same demands of our intellect; it should enable us to appreciate once more, as in a mirror, not only the Goodness of God but his Wisdom and his Power also.

Now, if we take the Gospel record as it stands; that is, if we consider the beliefs of first-century Christianity about the Life of its own Founder, dead twenty or thirty years ago, we shall find that this threefold chain of proof is fully represented. In the Personality of our Lord, or rather in his actions and words, which are all that remain to us of his Personality, we have seen the mirror of God's Goodness. In the fulfilment of Old Testament prophecy, which our chroniclers are at some pains to record, we shall see the mirror of his Wisdom. In the manifestations of supernatural Life which his miracles convey, we shall see the mirror of his Power. Let us consider the fulfilment of Old Testament prophecies first.

Like the argument from order in Nature, to which it corresponds, this argument from prophecy is somewhat out of favour in our day, chiefly because it has been pressed too far. It is not difficult to find "natural" explanations for some of the detailed correspondences between the Old Testament and the New. Thus, our Lord's action in riding into Jerusalem on an ass may be understood as the deliberate fulfilment, on his part, of certain Messianic conditions. The fact that the soldiers at the Crucifixion did actually "part among them the garments" of their Prisoner, need not be more than a coincidence. Or again, presuming the Evangelists to be capable of inaccuracies, Matthew's assertion that Judas received thirty pieces of silver for betraying his Master may be regarded as a mere legend, whose purpose was to make the facts fit the prophecy. On these, or some such principles as these, I suppose a resolute critic could account for all the texts in which the words "that it might be fulfilled which was spoken by the prophet" are found to occur.

But even if you eliminate the details, the broad fact remains—that Israel had been taught, through long centuries of history, to look forward to a Deliverer, and the Deliverer came; that he came at the moment when, it would appear, expectation was at its highest; that (as is clear from the acclamations which greeted him) he was popularly supposed to trace his descent from David; that he was believed to have performed miracles, such as those which were to usher in the Messiah's coming (Matthew 11:4,[2] cf. Isaias 35:5[3]); that he did call to himself a remnant, but only a remnant, of the people of Israel; that he did establish a "kingdom" in which the Gentiles found their true place; that his death was followed within a generation by the sack of Jerusalem (Daniel 9:26);[4] that his coming was immediately preceded by that of a prophet whose

[2] "And Jesus making answer said to them: Go and relate to John what you have heard and seen, etc."

[3] "Then shall the eyes of the blind be opened: And the ears of the deaf shall be unstopped."

[4] "And after sixty-two weeks Christ shall be slain: and the people that shall deny him shall not be his. And a people, with their leader that shall come, shall

life and character strongly resemble those of Elias, and so on. These are not texts chosen at random to suit a controversial purpose; they are integral elements in the current Messianic tradition which, if the Gospels are to be regarded as history at all, were notoriously verified in our Lord's career. If we could pronounce him an Impostor, we might suppose that he had contrived to achieve this reputation by artificial means. If we could write him down a Madman, we might suppose that he had been crazed by overmuch reading of apocalyptic literature, and had unconsciously come to live the part which his fancies suggested to him. As it is, are we not compelled to admit that there is a providential coincidence between Messianic prophecy and the actual career of him whom we worship as the Christ, significant enough to vindicate our belief in the Divine Foreknowledge? It is true, there was one element in our Lord's life which the popular expectation of his day did not anticipate—I mean, his sufferings and Death. But the latter, as we have seen, had been foretold by Daniel; and it is hard not to feel that his sufferings would equally have been foreseen, if the fifty-third chapter of Isaias had never found its way into the corpus of Messianic prophecy.

There remains the third element which we should expect to be present in an adequate Divine Revelation—the occurrence of miracles, the manifestation of Almighty Power. I do not mean that the inference, "Christ did miracles, therefore Christ is God", would be a legitimate one. We Catholics believe that God has used miracles to illuminate the career and to attest the mission of his saints, both under the Old and under the New Dispensation. The proof we derive from the Gospel miracles is that Almighty God would not have vindicated our Lord's career by such prodigies of Nature, if

destroy the city and the sanctuary: and the end thereof shall be waste, and after the end of the war the appointed desolation."

our Lord had been either a Deceiver or deceived as to his own Mission.

It is to be remembered that the Gospel records do not stand unsupported in their assertion that our Lord's coming was marked by extraordinary events. Those critics who glibly tell us that it is just as easy to understand miracles being falsely attributed to our Lord in the first century as to understand miracles being falsely attributed to St. Francis in the thirteenth, have curiously missed the point. Why did the thirteenth century so lightly credit St. Francis with miraculous powers? Because it was part of the tradition of the Church that saints do miracles. But how did that tradition arise? That tradition had been passed on continuosly from the first century, from the time of the apostles, *and there its parentage stops.* Belief in miracles (you may almost say) began, or at least began again, in the first century. The Jewish Scriptures record hardly any miracles after the time of the Captivity; there is no atmosphere of the miraculous to be found in Josephus, and the occultist claims of a Simon Magus only testify to a local and a personal influence. Pagans connected their stories of the miraculous only with antiquity; the very oracles were dumb at the time when our Lord came. And then suddenly, in this extraordinary first century, a blaze of credulity flares up through the world. There is no question of "ignorant peasants" merely; rich men like Barnabas, educated men like Paul, medical men like Luke, are suddenly swept away on this odd stream of belief in miracle. When the moderns say that "ignorant people are always expecting miracles to happen," what they really mean is that "ignorant *Christians* are always expecting miracles to happen." But there were no Christians till Christ came. When Christ came, people suddenly started believing in miracles—why?

The least that can reasonably be said is that our Lord's

lifetime was accompanied by certain events which—ignorantly, perhaps; stupidly, perhaps—people took to be supernatural events. You have a right to your own opinion, but do not deny that the strange events happened; that notion fails to account for this sudden outburst (if you will) of credulity which began in the first century and has continued ever since in the Christian Church.

Now, if we were convinced that our Lord was merely a Man, we might justify the patient process by which scholars go through the Gospel records, taking the miracles one by one, diagnosing faith cures here, coincidence there, mistaken medical analysis there, and so on; surmising that when our Lord seemed to be walking on the water he was really standing on a rock, and that when he fed the Five Thousand he only hypnotised them into supposing that they ate and were filled—the twelve baskets, even so, providing them with some embarrassment. But, since we have already seen that our Lord claimed to be God; since we have already seen the difficulties of supposing him to have been an impostor or a madman; since we have noted how curiously his career recalls the predictions of the Hebrew prophets, are we not, in hunting for these "natural" explanations, evading the obvious explanation—that the recorded miracles were real miracles, and that God, in his Omnipotence, saw fit to draw attention in this way to the career of his well-beloved Son? I can understand people having philosophic difficulties about miracles—I say "philosophic", not "scientific", for, *ex hypothesi*, the province of science is strictly limited to non-miraculous occurrences. I can understand people who do not believe in God's Omnipotence, or do not believe in his concurrence with the secondary causes we find in Nature, disbelieving in the *possibility* of miracles, and, since they believe them to be impossible, declaring (on curiously a priori grounds) that they never actually happen. I cannot understand people having historical difficulties about miracles. For, once you grant that miracles *can* happen, all the historical evidence at our disposal bids us believe that sometimes they do.

For economy of space, we can only direct particular attention to one of our Lord's miracles, though indeed it hardly falls into line with the rest; I mean, of course, his Resurrection. This has ever been the central issue in dispute; and, indeed, it is right that it should be so. Not only because it was the Resurrection, first and foremost, that the apostles preached, but because our Lord himself definitely constituted it a test case. "Destroy this temple, and in three days I will raise it up"—it is only John who records the context of this saying, but Matthew 26:61[5] is good corroboration of the fact. If we can trust the assumption implied by Matthew 27:62–63,[6] it was known to the Jewish leaders that a challenge to this effect had actually been issued. Even if no public challenge was issued, we have abundant evidence in the Synoptic Gospels that our Lord believed he would rise from the dead, prophesied it to his disciples, and treated the event as a fixed point in the future. It can hardly be wholesale misrepresentation of his teaching which has thrown his challenge so much into the foreground.

It is a plain fact that our Lord expected to rise from the dead; it is a plain fact that his Tomb was found empty on Easter morning. If we had no other evidence of this, we could infer it with practical certainty from Acts 2:29.[7] Whatever source Luke used for the early chapters of Acts, it is easy

[5] "And they said: This man said, I am able to destroy the temple of God and after three days to rebuild it."

[6] ". . . and the Pharisees came together to Pilate saying: Sir, we have remembered, that that seducer said, while he was yet alive: After three days I will rise again."

[7] "Ye men, brethren, let me freely speak to you of the patriarch David: that he died and was buried; and his sepulchre is with us to this present day, etc."

to see that the speeches there recorded, at least in their main outlines, are not "Thucydidean" speeches composed by the author, but are based on a genuine account of what was actually said. And the whole nerve of Peter's argument in Acts 2 is this: "The prophecy, Thou wilt not suffer thy Holy One to see corruption, cannot refer to David, because his sepulchre is still amongst us; therefore this prophecy must refer to Christ." Is it not plain that this logic includes a suppressed minor premise, "And, as you all know, the sepulchre of Jesus of Nazareth is *not* with us"? So Peter argues, less than two months after the Crucifixion, before an audience of whom many were dwellers at Jerusalem, and must have known the facts. Is it conceivable that he should have risked such an argument if it were not notorious that somehow, in whatever suspicious circumstances, the Tomb in which Jesus of Nazareth was buried was afterwards found empty?

The Empty Tomb, not the appearance of the Risen Christ, must be our point of departure; that is the fixed point. Accordingly, scholars have been busy these last hundred years trying to invent "natural" explanations of the circumstance. These attempts have failed with singular unanimity. They have traced the disappearance of the Body to Pilate, as if Pilate might have arranged its removal "in order to prevent a disturbance"—it is obvious, of course, that this would have been the worst possible way of securing his end; it would be precisely the disappearance of the Body which would *create* a disturbance. They have traced it to the Jews, who, of all people, were most intimately concerned to see that the Body was not stolen; who, of all people, would most willingly have produced the Body if it had been in their power to do so. They have told us that the holy women must have gone to the wrong tomb by mistake, as if it was likely (apart from what John tells us) that their amazing report was never verified!

The palpable futility of all these theories reflects admirably the bankruptcy of the criticism which produced them. Only one plausible theory of the kind has ever been devised, and it was devised immediately after the event; the Jews maintained that the Body had been secretly carried off by our Lord's own followers. Yet this is an explanation which no scholar has dared to adopt, for obvious reasons. Neither the psychology of the apostles at the time of the Passion, nor their psychology after the Resurrection, lends any colour to the idea that their whole story was a gigantic imposition, deliberately foisted on the world by a band of desperate devotees.

The earliest of the liberal critics had clearer vision. They saw that the Empty Tomb was a fact, and that there was only one explanation of the fact which a common-sense jury would look at for a moment—namely, that our Lord's Body left the Tomb, and left it alive. Accordingly they had recourse to the strangest expedients in attempting to prove that our Lord never died on the Cross. But, apart from its intrinsic improbability, we must take good note of what this theory involves. It means that Jesus of Nazareth, after escaping unharmed from the extreme penalty of the law, then and there set about the task of deluding posterity into the belief that he had died and risen again. Can we really believe that? Can we really reconcile that supposition with the estimate we have formed of his Character?

And yet, if you do not accept this conclusion, you have to explain away, not only the fact of the Empty Tomb, but also the fact of the Resurrection appearances. These have not been set out by any one Evangelist in a full, consecutive, historical form. Rather, it is clear that each missionary had a selected list of testimonies at his finger-ends. Paul actually runs through his own list at the beginning of 1 Corinthians 15. It looks as if someone, whether the author himself or a later editor, had used a similar list to fill in a gap, of memory or of manuscript, at the end of the second Gospel. So fragmentary is our knowledge, that we hear from two sources (Luke 24:34,[8] 1 Cor 15:5[9]) of a meeting between our Lord and St. Peter, which is nowhere described to us in its full context. The fact that the reminiscences preserved to us are preserved to us in so fragmentary a form is all the better proof of their authenticity. Plainly, the apostles never met and said, "We must have a story; what shall it be?" Plainly, no later editor with historical instincts has been through the evidence and tried to work it up into a brief. We are left with the naked testimony, such as it is, of first-hand witnesses.

The notion that these appearances were only visions is doubly false to history. It is false to the evidence, for in Matthew 28:9 the holy women take hold of our Lord's feet; in John 20:17 he says to Mary Magdalen, "Stop clinging to me"; in John 20:27 he invites the touch of an apostle; in Luke 24:30 and 43, Acts 1:4, he breaks bread and eats. It is as easy to discredit the evidence for our Lord's reappearance as to discredit the evidence for his reappearance in a physical form. And such a view is equally false to the economy of criticism; for it explains the Resurrection appearances on a principle which does not explain the Empty Tomb; it insists that our witnesses have made two separate mistakes, not one. Further, although these appearances were not continuous, but were spread over intervals during forty days (Acts 1:3)[10] it was clearly the impression of the first Christians that they depended upon the earthly presence of our Lord's natural Body, since they cease after its (alleged) Ascension; the experience

---

[8] "The Lord is risen indeed and hath appeared to Simon."

[9] "And that he was seen by Cephas; and after that by the eleven."

[10] "To whom also he shewed himself alive after his passion, by many proofs, for forty days appearing to them and speaking of the kingdom of God."

of Paul (1 Cor 15:8)[11] being clearly exceptional, and quoted as such. No further report has come down to us of our Lord as seen walking on earth; why not, unless the first Christians were convinced that it was a physical Body which appeared to them, and then disappeared?

It is to be remembered that, at best, historical evidence cannot produce mathematical certainty; it can only exclude reasonable doubt. It is to be remembered that an event which has no public, no political significance will be recorded only by unofficial documents; there will be no State record of the facts, no legal inquiry to establish them. It is to be remembered that, here if ever in the world's history, a miraculous event might be looked for—the vindication of a career so long expected in prophecy, of a Life so lived. And do we still find the story of the Resurrection fabulous? Shall we not rather reserve the epithet for the theories which scholarship has invented to explain it away?

[11] "And last of all he was seen also by me, as by one born out of due time."

X

Where Protestantism Goes Wrong

When we have come so far upon our journey, we have already parted company with a great portion of mankind; with the atheists, who deny God's existence, and with the pagans or pantheists, who misconceive his Nature; with the Jews, Mohammedans, and Unitarians, who refuse Divine honours to Jesus Christ. It is, if I may pursue my metaphor, at the very next turning that we have to take leave of our Protestant friends. For the next step on our journey is the step they never take. The next stage in our argument, after establishing the authority of Jesus Christ, is one which, if they are to be consistent with their own principles, they must needs disallow. We proceed immediately to the proof that our Lord Jesus Christ founded, before he left us, a single, visible, and invisible Church.

Before we proceed to that proof, it will be well to consider the consequences which are involved if we ignore it. I say, if we ignore it; for it is a matter of common experience that Protestants differ from us not so much because they disagree with us on this head, as because they refuse, most of them, to enter into the discussion at all. They are not clear-headed enough to perceive that a proper notion of the Church is a necessary stage before we argue from the authority of Christ to any other theological doctrine whatever. The infallibility of the Church is, for us, the true induction from which all our theological conclusions are derived. The Protestant, stopping short of it, has to rest content with an induction of the false kind; and the vice of that false kind of induction is that all its conclusions are already contained in its premises. Perhaps formal logic is out of date; let me restate the point otherwise. We derive from our apprehension of the living Christ the apprehension of a living Church; it is from that living Church that we take our guidance. Protestantism claims to take its guidance immediately from the living Christ. But what is the guidance he gives us, and where are we to find it? That is the question over which Protestantism has always failed to answer the Catholic challenge, over which it finds it increasingly difficult, nowadays, to answer the challenge of its own children.

We may be pardoned, perhaps, for making a distinction here in parenthesis. Protestants, especially old-fashioned Protestants, often talk as if, for Catholics, the Church came between Christ and the soul. That is a falsehood; only ignorance can excuse them for repeating it. For the Catholic, as for the Protestant, sanctification is the direct work of Christ; it is Christ, not the Church, who gives us (as Priest and as Victim) his Body and Blood in Communion. It is Christ who forgives us our sins, sometimes when we submit them to the Church in Confession, sometimes before. The Catholic, no less than the Protestant, hopes to be saved through the merits of Christ's Blood shed for him, and for no other consideration. The Church, then, in the order of worship, does not come between Christ and the individual soul. But in the order of intellectual conviction, the Church does, if you will, come between Christ and the individual mind. It is through the

Church that the Catholic finds out what he is to believe and why he is to believe it.

The argument we have pursued in the last nine chapters is one which would have commended itself, I suppose, to all Protestants in the days when Protestantism began. The existence of God, the proofs of it, the Omnipotence of God, the authority of Christ, and the proofs of that, from his own Character, from the fulfilment of prophecy, and from the witness of his miracles—all this would have been fully endorsed by those sturdy controversialists, the seventeenth-century Anglican divines. With what follows in the succeeding chapters they must perforce have disagreed, for it reduces the rest of Christian doctrine to an inference from the authority of the Church. And let it not be said that Anglicans have professed and still profess some sort of reverence for "the authority of the Church". The Church, for Catholics, is a visible fact; for Protestants it is an intellectual figment.

For three centuries the true issue between the two parties was obscured, owing to the preposterous action of the Protestants in admiring Biblical inspiration. The Bible, it appeared, was common ground between the combatants, the Bible, therefore, was the arena of the struggle; from it the controversialist, like David at the brook, must pick up texts to sling at his adversary. In fact, of course, the Protestant had no conceivable right to base any arguments on the inspiration of the Bible, for the inspiration of the Bible was a doctrine which had been believed, before the Reformation, on the mere authority of the Church; it rested on exactly the same basis as the doctrine of Transubstantiation. Protestantism repudiated Transubstantiation, and in doing so repudiated the authority of the Church; and then, without a shred of logic, calmly went on believing in the inspiration of the Bible, as if nothing had happened! Did they suppose that

Biblical inspiration was a self-evident fact, like the axioms of Euclid? Or did they derive it from some words of our Lord? If so, what words? What authority have we, apart from that of the Church, to say that the Epistles of Paul are inspired, and the Epistle of Barnabas is not? It is, perhaps, the most amazing and the most tragic spectacle in the history of thought, the picture of blood flowing, fires blazing, and king-doms changing hands for a century and a half, all in defence of a vicious circle.

The only logic which succeeded in convincing the Protes-tants of their fallacy was the logic of facts. So long as nobody except scoffers and atheists challenged the truth of the scrip-tural narratives, the doctrine of inspiration maintained its curiously inflated credit. Then Christians, nay, even clergy-men, began to wonder about Genesis, began to have scruples about the genuineness of 2 Peter. And then, quite suddenly, it became apparent that there was no reason why Protestants should not doubt the inspiration of the Bible; it violated no principle of their system. The Evangelicals protested, but theirs was a sentimental rather than a reasoned protest; the Tractarians fulminated, but it was plain this was mere summer lightning, a reflection from the Seven Hills. Only the con-demnation of Colenso stands as monument of the bloodless victory of Modernism. For three centuries the inspired Bible had been a handy stick to beat Catholics with; then it broke in the hand that wielded it, and Protestantism flung it lan-guidly aside.

I do not mean, of course, that modern Protestants do not affirm, and affirm sincerely, their belief in Biblical inspiration *of some sort*. But if you examine the affirmation, you will find that the whole meaning of the term has changed; it was once a literal inspiration that was acknowledged, now it is only a literary inspiration. If you need tangible proof of this, you have only to consider the amount of literary flattery which is lavished upon certain Biblical authors by modern scholar-ships; how they belaud the fierce independence of Amos, the profound spiritual insight of St. Paul. It was all one to our great-grandfathers; Amos, for them, was no more of a figure than Habacuc, or Paul than the author of the Apocalypse; what did it matter? It was all inspired.

The consequences of this change in the Protestant attitude towards Scripture did not become apparent at once. In the days of Westcott and Lightfoot, in the days of Salmon, the impression left on the public was that it did not matter much whether the Bible was inspired, because in any case it was true. Westcott said so, and who more likely to know than Westcott? Salmon said so; and he was not the man to commit himself to a rash judgment. The prevailing tone in English scholarship remained conservative, at least so far as the New Testament was concerned; books were still attributed to their traditional authors, their integrity was maintained in defiance of the innovators, legend was not allowed to obtrude itself as a hypothesis. If we kept to Codex Vaticanus we should be all right.

In our time, we are beginning to reap the whirlwind. Even men of moderate opinions will not, today, vouch for the authenticity of the Fourth Gospel; will not quote the three-fold invocation of Matthew 28:19 [1] as certainly representing the views of the apostolic age; will not attach any importance to the story of our Lord's Ascension. And these things are done in the green tree; what of the dry? If these are the hesitations which Protestantism cultivates, what of those it tolerates? We have seen in our time Oxford—the Oxford that flamed with controversy over the case of Dr. Hampden—

---

[1] "Going therefore, teach ye all nations: baptizing them in the name of the Father and of the Son and of the Holy Ghost."

vaguely discussing whether anything could be done about a clergyman who denied the Resurrection.

I do not mean to suggest, what these criticisms might at sight appear to suggest, that Biblical study, unguided by any belief in the doctrines of a teaching Church, is certain to lead men to wrong conclusions. I mean that such study is humanly certain to lead different men to different conclusions, even on subjects of the highest moment. If they belonged to a living Church, its traditions, or its instincts, the unconscious fruit of its traditions, would act as a corrective; one view would be ruled out as inadequate. "No," the Church would say, "my child, the Evangelist cannot have meant that." The dead letter and the living instinct support and correct one another. But the Protestant critics have no such arbiter to adjudge their theological awards; two different doctrines are held, and therefore neither doctrine is certain. I have already attempted, in Chapter 1, to give some picture of the confusion which these embarrassments have introduced; but perhaps it will be well for the sake of clearness to give here two concrete instances of the kind of hesitation I refer to.

No question could be more acute in the modern world than the question whether Christian marriage can or cannot be dissolved. A Church which has any claim to guide the consciences of its subjects may reasonably be expected to have a definite view for or against; or at least to have some hard-and-fast definition of the circumstances in which dissolution is possible. Consulted on the matter, the Protestant theologian of today must perforce turn to the historical records of the earliest Christianity, and find out what are supposed to have been our Lord's views on the subject. (The result of such inquiries is not always so clear as might have been expected; it is sufficient to recall the very curious pronouncement made by Luther in answer to the Landgrave of Hesse.) According to

Mark 10:11, "Whosoever shall put away his wife and marry another, committeth adultery against her"; the same statement is to be found in Luke 16:18. On the other hand, in Matthew 5:32, a reservation is apparently made, "except it be for the cause of fornication", and again in Matthew 19:9. The exception is not quoted by St. Paul (1 Cor 7:10). Is it then permissible for an "innocent party" to remarry?

How comes it (the theologian must ask himself) that two separate forms of what is apparently the same dictum have been preserved to us? Did one stand originally in Mark, and the other in "Q"? And, if so, which of those two sources is the earlier, which is the more reliable? What are the chances that an editor of lax views has tampered with the text in Matthew, an editor of strict views has tampered with the text in Mark? Does the exception offer relief only to the man, or to the woman in like case? What confirmation does the text from St. Paul lend to the stricter view? At best, an appeal to him may be represented as a precarious argument from silence. Does the word "put away" imply full divorce or mere legal separation? And finally (a point to which too little attention has been directed), is it certain that the phrases which are translated "except for the cause of fornication" really bear that meaning in the original Greek? On all this the theologians have to decide; and, if you shut them up in a committee room, it is fairly certain that you will be left with a majority and a minority report. Meanwhile, here is the happiness of two lives (in the modern jargon) awaiting a unanimous decision. How is it possible for Protestantism to offer a united front to their eager questioning?

In practice, of course, the stricter view has hitherto been favoured by Anglican pronouncements. Conservatism, the fear of setting up precedents, the fear of angry protests in High Church quarters, weigh heavily in the scale. But the point is not whether a Protestant tribunal can return a definite answer on the point, but whether it has any *right* to return a definite answer; whether it can expect any confidence to be felt in the award given, any attention to be paid to it. The evidence is at least sufficiently obscure to allow of a "probable opinion" in favour of the innocent party; and, according to the recognised principles of moral theology, a probable opinion may be followed. We must not confuse the power to enforce decisions with the right to make them.

Or again, you may consider the bearing of this difficulty even on a purely doctrinal, not a disciplinary point. The question whether there is or is not eternal punishment for impenitent sinners beyond the grave is one, surely, which a revelation might have been expected to settle for us. It is a belief which has been constantly affirmed by the Church; it is a belief which Protestants found no difficulty in accepting, so long as Protestants believed in the inerrancy of the Bible. On the other hand, it is a belief which seems to most free-thinkers in our day a superstition, and a superstition which taxes Almighty God with systematic cruelty. There could hardly be a subject on which, you would think, a preacher would be more anxious to deliver a clear message, one way or the other. Once again let us remit the question to the tribunal of Protestant scholarship; what is the verdict?

Here it must be confessed that the common-sense inquirer would be disposed to say that the words of the Gospel left our Lord's sentiments in no kind of doubt. "To be cast into Gehenna, where their worm does not die, and the fire is not quenched", "Depart from me, ye wicked, into the everlasting fire which is prepared for the devil and his angels"—such language might be considered plain enough, yet not all scholars are convinced by these apparently unequivocal declarations. One will say that the words must be understood metaphorically; another, that our Lord was accommodating his expressions to suit the notions of his own day; another, that those who reported his words have misrepresented him, and so on. So long as these rival possibilities hold the field, there can be no certainty whether hell is a fact or not. Those who assert the doctrine can only assert it as a pious opinion, and at the risk of finding their preaching flatly contradicted by bishops of their own communion.

It will be objected, however, that contemporary Anglicanism, whatever the practice of the other Christian bodies, does not confine itself to this Scriptural appeal. Many, at all events, of its most distinguished apologists supplement this appeal to the Bible—that is, to the critics of the Bible—by an appeal to the Church—that is, to the historians of the Church. The Anglicans of the seventeenth century, the Tractarians of the nineteenth century, pointed us to the first six centuries of Christendom as authoritative; others would point us to the first thirteen, the first fifteen, or even the first eighteen, but the difference is one of detail; it is not the Church, but the history of the Church that we are invited by these controversialists to accept as the criterion of orthodoxy. But this fresh appeal involves us in fresh embarrassments, no less serious than those already mentioned. Let us tabulate them for convenience—

1. In the first place, those who make this appeal are not always prepared to abide by it in matters of detail. There is no record in Christian antiquity of priests being allowed to marry after ordination; yet many of those who make this appeal have themselves married under the conditions mentioned, and all of them are committed to the defence of a Church which tolerates such marriages. Can we really feel any great veneration for a principle of authority which, in practice, is so inconsistently applied?

2. The appeal to the Church of the Historians, like the appeal to the Bible of the Critics, is one which fails to produce certainty. No subject, I suppose, could have been more carefully investigated by Christian scholars than the history of the ministry—had the Church originally bishops as part of its constitution, or only priests and deacons? Even on such a question, Presbyterian scholars still find room for disagreement with their Anglican brethren. Auricular confession, which is preached as obligatory by some Anglicans, cannot be traced to the primitive Church with a certainty which would convince all historians. Even doctrines such as that of the Trinity or that of the two Natures in the Incarnation appear in a strictly defined form only in the third or fourth century. Now, it is true that you escape from these particular difficulties by appealing to six centuries instead of one or two; but who told you that there should be six, no less and no more? Is it a mystical number, that it should be credited with this strange finality?

3. But the essential weakness of this appeal to antiquity is that it resolutely shuts its eyes to the really salient fact about Christendom; I mean that it was essentially *one*. The unity and the uniqueness of the Christian Church are assumed in the language of its writers from the very earliest times of which we have record. St. Ignatius sees in the local bishop the representative of that college of bishops scattered throughout the world, whose unity is the unity of the faith. St. Paul, writing in days when it would hardly seem possible that heresies should have become a serious threat, stigmatises heretics as having made shipwreck of the faith, and urges his converts to abide in the unity of the doctrine. The modern Christianities, be they what they may, are the relics of schism; not one of them dares to represent itself as the one Church of Christ. Consequently, in appealing to the early Church, with

its instinct of inviolable unity, they are appealing to an arbiter who has already given the award against them.

May the innocent party remarry after divorce? It may indeed be possible, in this particular instance, to show that there is no proof of any such practice having been tolerated by the early Church. But the early Church, judged by the same standards, cannot be proved to have allowed the marriage of ordained priests. If we do not respect the voice of Christian antiquity when it makes the priesthood a bar to matrimony, why should we respect the voice of Christian antiquity when it makes previous wedlock a bar to matrimony? But worse is to follow.

In the last verses of Ephesians 5, St. Paul bases the doctrine of Christian marriage upon the doctrine of Christ's Union with his Church. In our day, men will believe that a husband must only have one wife, yet deny that Christ has only one Church. I do not mean that they will formally deny it; they will tell you that for them "the Church" means something greater and wider than any defined body of Christians. But their actions and the position which they occupy have the effect of perpetuating a schism by which part of Christendom was torn away from Church unity. They believe with the early Christians that marriage is indissoluble; they will not believe with the early Christians that the Church is indivisible.

The propaganda of Tractarianism and of Post-Tractarianism has had its successes, and will have its successes, by opening up new devotional opportunities to a nation starved for lack of spiritual enthusiasm. It will never claim intellectual respect from the outside view until it can persuade us to overlook this fatal flaw in its own title-deeds. Its champions appeal to the undivided Church, and yet expect the undivided Church to overlook their division from it. They suppose that for so many centuries—six, or thirteen, or fifteen, or eighteen—

the Holy Spirit guided its councils, and then deserted it. And of this weakness in their own appeal they are beginning to show consciousness. They no longer take the lead, as they did fifty years ago, in the battle for traditional orthodoxy; they are ready to condone the infidelities of their fellow-churchmen, as long as they themselves are left in peace. The salt has lost its savour, and the corruption of non-Catholic theology continues.

There is, however, one Christian body in the world which, till recently, showed no signs of this theological disintegration, and which might yet, by a determined effort, repel its influences; I mean that federation of national churches around the Levant (with an outcrop in Russia) which goes by the name of the Orthodox Church. It is hard to prophesy its future; political alliances have ever been its besetting temptation, and, with the breakdown of Tsarism in Russia, it has shown an increasing tendency to fraternise with the Protestant denominations of the East. If this tendency wins, there can be little doubt that the Orientals will sell their birthright of orthodoxy for a mess of pottage. But that orthodoxy is itself due, rather to the intense conservatism which has shielded them even from liturgical development, than to any theory of ecclesiastical authority. Orders they have, and sacraments, but they have no better claim to be a teaching Church than have the Christianities of the West. They, too, broke away from the unity of the Church; for them, as for the Protestants, undivided Christendom is a memory in the past, a figment in the present, a dream of the future; not a living reality as it is for us. They preferred to have their own way; and he who has once made that choice will labour in vain to impress his authority upon others.

I have only tried to deal with the broadest outlines of a controversy necessarily confused. Necessarily confused, because the Protestant case has been presented to the world at different times and by different authors with a thousand ingenious refinements which have made it a special study in apologetic. It would be intensely wearisome to the general reader if, in a book of this scope, he were asked to follow all the intricate mazes of a dispute which is now four centuries old, and has lost some of its bitterness without losing its obscurity. We Catholics have always taken our stand on a simple principle, that which is to be expounded in the following chapter; it is not our fault if the ingenuity of others has darkened counsel. The fact remains that in our day Protestantism is losing its character in all the Protestant countries; from what causes, it must be left to the reader to judge.

XI

The Foundation of the Church

What did our Lord leave behind him at his Ascension? An example, certainly, to the human race; but you need not be a Christian to inherit that. He left behind him no writings; the Scriptures of the New Testament were composed years later, and it is the Church, not our Lord personally, that guarantees to us their authenticity and their integrity. He left behind him a body of moral precepts, and something, at least, of a theology. But all these, be it observed, have only been handed down to us by the agency of a society which he originated; a society which consisted in the first instance of his own immediate followers. That society is primarily his legacy to the world; he left us, not Christianity, but Christendom.

It was expected among the Jews that a Messiah would come to earth, and would set up something vaguely described as a kingdom. In this kingdom not the whole people of the Jews, but a remnant of them, would take part; what effect it would have upon the Gentile world was not clear, but it was clear that the Gentile world would be somehow interested. It was not certain whether the kingdom would be an earthly kingdom simply, or whether it would be preceded by a Resurrection, and would thus constitute a new world-order altogether. It was generally imagined that it would appear suddenly; and it was confidently believed that under its benign influence all traces of crime, cruelty, and unhappiness would disappear. To what extent did our Lord endorse this popular expectation of the kingdom; to what extent did he correct it?

He certainly declared his intention of founding a kingdom; indeed, I suppose it would be almost true to say that the greater part of his teaching as recorded in the Synoptic Gospels is immediately concerned with it. It is clear that he did not refer to a political institution, for he invariably refused to be identified with any political agitation. Yet this kingdom was to be on earth, not in heaven; for the Resurrection was to take place at the end of it, not at the beginning of it. It is compared to the sowing of a crop, and the end of the world is to be the harvest; to the lowering of a net, and the end of the world is to be the landing of the catch; to the departure of a king into a far country, and the end of the world is to be his return. Further, this kingdom is not to be (as the Jews supposed) a millennium; there will be tares as well as wheat in the harvest, good as well as bad fish in the catch—righteous men and sinners, that is to say, will continue to live side by side in his kingdom as before it.

This kingdom of his is not to appear suddenly. Recent scholars have sometimes imagined that our Lord expected his own death to be followed by some sudden world-catastrophe, which would usher in a new order of things, and that this new order was the "kingdom" referred to. But he has been careful to explain that his kingdom is a slow growth, which you might compare to the action of a man who plants a mustard seed, or that of a woman who hides leaven in three measures of meal. So far from encouraging his followers to think that a world-catastrophe is to be expected shortly, he goes out of his way to assure them that a long period of waiting must precede it; and that period of waiting will be his kingdom. The householder must sleep and rise night and day while the seed grows; it is a far country that the king is visiting, and his return from it is delayed.

Thus the kingdom may be identified with a period of time; that period of time, namely—our Lord will not specify its length—which is to intervene between its institution and his coming again. But the kingdom may also be viewed as a collection of people, the "remnant" of which the prophets had spoken. Are these people to be Jews and Gentiles, or only Jews? Under a multitude of comparisons our Lord announces that Gentiles as well as Jews will be members of it. The Elder Son must not suppose that he has inherited his patrimony to the exclusion of the Prodigal; the labourers who have been long at work in the vineyard must not repine at the equal treatment offered to the late-comers. In fact, the kingdom will consist predominantly of Gentiles, since the obstinacy of the Jews will lose them their chance of finding their proper place in it. The guests who were first invited are replaced by poor men from the highways and hedges; the beggar Lazarus is preferred to Dives; the Wicked Husbandmen will be miserably destroyed, and the vineyard will be given over to others. As a race, the Jews are excluded from the privileges of the kingdom. Many are called, but few are chosen—among the Jews, that is, the people who expect to be called.

The whole notion, then, which became popular in Reformation times, that "the Church" which our Lord left behind him was not a group of persons bound together by marks of external unity, but simply the sum total (known only to God) of those souls which were actually destined to achieve eternal life—all that notion is an afterthought and a chimæra. So is any notion of the Church which would credit it with a merely ideal, not with a visible and external unity. The Calvinistic idea is sufficiently refuted by the parables themselves, by the existence of tares among the wheat, worthless fish among the catch, foolish virgins among the bridal party. But indeed, that the Church our Lord contemplated in the first instance was a "visible" not an "invisible" Church is sufficiently attested by the very circumstances of its foundation. It was not a foundation, strictly speaking, but a refoundation.

A Church of God had been in existence ever since the time of Moses. The Ecclesia, the Assembly of the Jews, had been a selection (that is what the word implies) from amongst all the nations of the world. The Ecclesia, the Assembly of Christ, was a further selection from among the Jews themselves—he came to save a "remnant", as we have seen above. Into this new Ecclesia, it is true, he drafted a great quantity of Gentile believers; but primarily the Ecclesia of Christ is a further selection from the Ecclesia of God, itself a selection from the peoples of the world. He speaks of it as "my Ecclesia" as opposed to the old Ecclesia of his Father. The solidarity of this new Assembly could no longer, *ex hypothesi*, be a merely national solidarity. But the new Assembly was a collection of persons, bound together by external marks of unity, no less than the old; there is no word in our Lord's teaching which implies any change of policy in this respect.

And as the nucleus around which this new Assembly should cohere he chose with infinite prudence, trained with infinite care, a little body of disciples, who were to be the witnesses of his Resurrection. It is extraordinary, to anybody who will read the Gospel with his eyes open, how much of our Lord's teaching, even of his recorded teaching, is addressed not to the multitudes who flocked to hear him, but to the little band of followers who were continually in his society. These are the people who are to represent him after he is gone; they will be persecuted as he has been persecuted before them; they will have to stand before princes and governors in the strength with which his own Spirit will supply them. Nay, he has actually reserved for them the privilege of evangelising the world; himself, he is sent to the lost sheep of the house of Israel, and it is only with reluctance that he will go outside his own country, or relieve the necessities of a Gentile suppliant. All through his ministry his thoughts seem to be centred on their ministry, which is to be the posthumous continuation of his own.

Accordingly, he is always at pains to impress them with a sense of their special dignity. They are to be fishers of men, bringing souls into the Net of his Kingdom. They are the salt of the earth, destined to preserve it from the corruption which threatens to destroy it. They are a city set on a hill— with such a lonely solidarity does he credit them. Their ministry, surely, is that of the inn-keeper to whom the Good Samaritan entrusts his wounded guest. They are the scattered reapers of a plenteous harvest. To them it is given to know the secrets of the kingdom. They are the new bottles into which the new wine must be poured. They in their own way, as he in his, are the light which is to enlighten the world. Their number has been chosen so as to correspond to that of the twelve tribes of Israel. And after his Resurrection, in a well-known passage at the end of the first Gospel, he deliberately devolves upon them the authority committed to him by his Heavenly Father. "All power is given to ME; going, therefore, teach YE all nations." It is hard to see what words he could have found to express more strongly the continuation of his own mission in theirs.

Our Lord, then, contemplated the foundation of a visible Church, and as the nucleus of that Church he left behind him a little group of apostles authorised to act in his name. We know something of the instructions which he gave them; they date either from the end of his life or from the interviews he had with them after the Resurrection. They were to baptise; they were to continue the Memorial of his own Death which he left to them before his Passion; they had power to forgive sins—the very power which the Pharisees would have denied to himself. When we hear in Acts 1:3 that "he showed himself . . . for forty days, appearing to them and speaking of the kingdom of God", we are doubtless to understand that these recorded injunctions do not exhaust the scope of his oral commission. Much that he said has not been preserved to us; to guess at its nature, we must observe the behaviour of the apostles themselves a few days after his Ascension into Heaven.

From the very outset of the Acts, you have the impression that the Church has sprung into being ready-made. Not that it has no lessons to learn from experience, needs no fresh revelations to guide it. But it knows already how to deal with each fresh situation that arises, and does so with a wonderful sureness of touch. The apostles, who owe their appointment to the command of a Divine Voice, have no hesitation in co-opting a fresh apostle on their own responsibility. They set aside, on their own responsibility, seven men to act in a newly created capacity as deacons. On both these occasions the multitude of the Church, being then a compact body, is directed to proceed to an election; but it is the apostles who lay their hands on the newly ordained deacons to invest them with their sacred character. This imposition of hands (nowhere prescribed by our Lord in any recorded utterance) appears, in early apostolic practice as a normal supplement to the ceremony of baptism. About twenty years after the Ascension, an Apostolic Council decides, once more on its own responsibility, what respect is to be shown, in areas where Judaism is strong, to the scruples of Jewish Christians. There is nothing amateurish, nothing haphazard in all this procedure; it reflects, surely, the administrative instincts of a self-contained and self-conscious institution.

Let it be remembered that we have no reason to suspect the presence in the Church, at this stage of its existence, of any commanding intellect, any organising genius. Its administrators are the same fishermen whom we met in the Gospels; they are still unlearned and ignorant men in the world's eyes. Is it credible that this peaceful, orderly development should not have been in line with the expressed intentions of their Founder? Is it not plain that the Acts form a history spiritually continuous with the Gospels; and that the continuity of a single organised body, the Christian Church, which can easily be traced to the period of the Acts, is thus traceable to our Lord himself? It seems hard to believe that anything except special pleading on the part of disappointed minorities could have brought the fact into question.

Two points, however, remain to be discussed. What is the value of the instinct which the Church certainly has today, and seems to have had at all times, that the guidance of its Ascended Master was constantly with it to protect it from error? And, given that at any period of history a dispute should arise, in which two parties within the Church claimed severally to be the supporters of orthodox tradition, on what permanent principle can such a dispute be settled?

Nobody, I take it, will question the existence of this instinct; few will question its primitive character. When St. Paul tells the Ephesians that they are built upon the foundation of the apostles and prophets, Jesus Christ being himself the chief corner-stone, it can hardly be doubted that he refers to the edifice of their faith, in the sense of intellectual belief. In no other way do the apostles and prophets act as a medium between Christ and the Christian soul. In another epistle, the first to Timothy, he identifies the Church of God as the pillar and ground of truth, using the same metaphor with even more precise application. And indeed the reason for this confidence becomes explicit in the decree sent out by the Council of Jerusalem in Acts 15—in the circumstances, it can hardly be otherwise than authentic—"It hath seemed good to the Holy Ghost and to us." A decision of the Church, however stormy the discussion which has preceded it, is assumed to be the decision of the Holy Spirit. Had the early Christians no ground for such a conviction?

Anyone who believes that the Fourth Gospel is, not necessarily an authentic record, but an authentic echo of our Lord's personal teaching, can hardly doubt whence this confidence arose. The metaphor of the True Vine plainly conceives the Church as an organic institution, living with a common life; and it is to this institution, not to a prophet here and a teacher there, that those momentous promises are made—the gift of the Holy Spirit, his teaching office, his perpetual presence as something more than the Representative of our Lord himself. But indeed, such language is anticipated in the Synoptic Gospels; it is the Holy Spirit who is to put speech into the apostles' mouths when they stand before princes and governors; it is in virtue of his inspiration that they are empowered to forgive and to retain sins. Predominantly in the New Testament the Holy Spirit is conceived as communicated, not to the individual soul, but to the Body which he energises and organises, the Church of Christ. And this gift of inspiration means the permanent presence of our Lord himself with his Church; in sending out his apostles to teach, he reminds them that he is with them all days, even to the consummation of the world.

It is to be remembered that such permanent guidance, sufficient to preserve the Church from all danger of serious error, is essential to the very conditions of a revelation. We must repeat it, our Lord left behind him no syllable of writing; he committed, therefore, wholly to his Church the task of representing him, and not misrepresenting him, before the world. If he had been merely human, like the other founders of religious sects, he would have had to take his chance of misrepresentation, trusting in the general loyalty of his immediate followers. A comparison of modern Lutheranism with Luther, or of modern Anglicanism with Cranmer, will show at a glance how ill such confidence is reposed. Would it not be natural to assume, even if his own language had given us no justification for the assumption, that he who came to earth in order to bestow upon us a final revelation of God, would see to it that his purposes were not frustrated by infidelity on the part of his legatees?

He would not, however, altogether override the shortcomings of human nature. He would leave his Church providentially guaranteed from error, but he would not guarantee that no member of it, no body of Christians, should ever be allowed to stray from the straight path of his teaching. Such errors, granted sufficient obstinacy in those who propound them, will necessarily lead to ecclesiastical disputes; such disputes will mean that one party is in the right and the other in the wrong; but how are we to know, how is posterity to know, which party is in the right and which party is in the wrong? Some principle of arbitration must be present from the first, if these disputes are to be adequately settled. Three possible methods of arbitration might suggest themselves—

1. The Divine Teacher, who based his own claim to human allegiance partly on the miracles which he performed, might

conceivably have left this power of performing miracles to his true Church, by way of distinguishing it from all false churches, all schismatic sects. In a sense, our Lord did do this. "These signs shall follow them that believe; in my name they shall cast out devils; they shall lay hands on the sick, and they shall recover", and so on. Moreover, it is observable that St. Paul does, once at least, appeal to this principle of adjudication, when his own apostleship has been called in question. A comparison of verse 3 with verse 10 of 2 Corinthians 13 indicates, surely, that the fate of Ananias in Acts 5 was not an isolated warning. And the Catholic Church has always claimed that the persistence of ecclesiastical miracles is a subsidiary proof of her own legitimacy. But it is obvious that if miracle-working were the sole test of orthodoxy, a profusion of miracles would be necessary if all men in every age were to have the chance of judging which was the true Church. Some other touchstone, then, must be found by which error can be distinguished from truth.

2. It would be most natural, perhaps, in our day to suppose that the democratic principles of majorities, counting heads to avoid breaking them, would be the proper way of settling ecclesiastical as of settling civil disputes. No suggestion of such a principle is to be found in the New Testament; that is perhaps natural, since the heresies of the time were probably small and local heresies. Here again, the Catholic Church claims that she can justify her own position by an appeal to majorities; there has been no recognised council at which the Catholic side was not preponderant; and it is doubtful whether there has ever been a majority of bishops in disagreement with the Holy See in any matter of controversy, even when the Oriental dioceses were in a state of half-rebellion. It seems equally clear that at any period of history at which even rough statistics are available, the

Catholics, I mean the Christians in Communion with the Holy See, had outnumbered those who took the opposite side in the question under dispute. But such numerical tests are at once undignified and unsatisfactory. They open the way to all the jobbery and intrigue of the committee-room. Likely enough, in the order of Divine Providence, that at any time of schism the faithful should preponderate in numbers. But is it to be expected that they should wait to see whether they preponderate in numbers or no, before they declare for this side or for that?

3. Failing either of these two tests, it remains that the unity of the Church should be secured against schism by some form, however modified, however ill-defined, of monarchical succession. In the long run, one man has one voice; and it would be difficult work to ascertain what we call, by a metaphor, the Voice of the Church, if there were not one particular man in the world whose single voice could be identified with the sentiments of Christendom. This system of securing perpetuity by personal succession is of course a common feature of religious history; sometimes there will be a family succession, like the Khalifate or the Kings of England, sometimes a spiritual succession like that of the Grand Lamas. We are the less familiar with it because in our own day most of the denominations owe their ultimate solidarity to their title-deeds. In times when religions have no legal status as bodies corporate, the monarchical principle is the natural one; it secures that at any given moment there shall be one man who has the last word in any case of dispute. It would be no anachronism, no unprecedented action, if our Lord should have determined to appoint such a single, undying official in his own Church, the centre of its cohesion and the arbiter of its possible controversies. And if so (it must be observed from the first), that guidance which protects the Church from error

must, a fortiori, protect from error the one mind which is to be umpire in case of a disagreement.

If our Lord (let us indulge the fancy) had wished to appoint such a personal representative to be the leader, the spokesman, and in the last resort the arbiter, of his infant Church, upon whom should we naturally have expected his choice to light, from what we know of his immediate followers? There can be no two answers to such a question. There is one apostle whose name occurs in some sixty contexts scattered over the four Gospels (no other achieves more than twenty-five mentions); one apostle who is constantly, you may say invariably, the spokesman of the rest, who takes the initiative at every crisis, who is distinguished (Mark 16:7)[1] by our Lord himself as holding, somehow, a unique position, and was actually the first apostle to whom he appeared after his Resurrection. Whatever else is certain about the Gospel tradition, it is certain that the name of Simon Peter is deeply imbedded in its structure.

If our Lord did appoint such a personal representative, we should expect him to figure prominently in the early history of the Church. And indeed, the first twelve chapters of the Acts are a kind of epic of St. Peter; everywhere he takes the lead, almost everywhere he is the hero. When he leaves Jerusalem he leaves the story; yet he reappears at the Council of Jerusalem; in the discussion proper he speaks first—the position of honour in all ancient assemblies—and perhaps calms the doubts of his more Judaising colleague St. James. Once in the epistles we find him criticised, where his respect for the scruples of certain Judaising brethren brings upon him a somewhat un-Pauline rebuke from St. Paul; yet even here it is

---

[1] "But go, tell his disciples and Peter that he goeth before you into Galilee."

observable that his lead is followed by Barnabas, and that the Apostle of the Gentiles congratulates himself upon an unusual display of independence. Meanwhile, it appears that as far off as Corinth Peter's name is familiar enough to be the watch-word of a party; and (if the first epistle that bears his name is genuine, or represents a genuine tradition) he addressed his exhortations to the whole area now known as Asia Minor.

We all know the passage (in Matthew 16) in which our Lord does actually confer on Peter this unique position— perhaps some non-Catholics would be the better for rereading it with a little care; familiarity stales the sensational. Whether it was modesty, or prudence, or some other cause that silenced Mark, Peter's own disciple, on this subject, it is not necessary to inquire; it could hardly have been possible for Matthew to foist this passage into his Gospel if it did not record a fact. (Mark, it may be observed, records in 10:35 [2] the consequent jealousy of Zebedee's sons.) Nor can we suspect interpolation; the contrast between "rock" in verse 18 and "stone of offence" in verse 23 shows that it is all part of one story. In this passage, then, our Lord calls Simon (or the faith which he shows) "a Rock", using the same metaphor under which he refers to himself in Mark 12:10.[3] He declares his intention of founding his Church on this rock, impregnable against the powers of evil. He promises to him the keys of the Church, his kingdom; a comparison with Isaias 22:22 [4] will show the measure of confidence which this metaphor implies. He also promises to him individually a power of binding

[2] "And James and John, the sons of Zebedee, came to him, saying: Master, we desire that whatsoever we shall ask, thou wouldst do it for us."

[3] "And have you not read this scripture, *The stone which the builders rejected, the same is made the head of the corner.*"

[4] "And I will lay the key of the house of David upon his shoulder: and he shall open and none shall shut: and he shall shut and none shall open."

and loosing, which is doubtless to be shared in some sense by the rest of the apostles. Has anybody ever read a Protestant interpretation of this passage without being conscious of scholarship in difficulties?

In Luke 22:32 another utterance is recorded, "When thou hast returned, be a support to thy brethren", which is significant enough when it comes as a pendant to the words "I have prayed for thee that thy strength fail not"—it is the only record we have of our Lord offering prayer for an individual. Does not this, too, help to define Peter's relation to his fellow-apostles? And finally, in John 21, after deliberately singling out Peter among his fellows, our Lord devolves upon him that pastoral office which was his own prized title in Chapter 10. Can we doubt that, though the plenitude of authority has been put in commission among the apostles, the plenitude of apostleship lies here?

On the whole, modern Protestant writers are disposed to admit so much, and to reserve their doubts for the next stage in our argument. Granted that Peter held this unique position, did it pass on from him to the bishops of Rome? To which our most natural answer is, If not to them, to whom? For, surely, promises so momentous as those just quoted are out of all proportion to their subject if they were made to an individual as an individual. Did Peter really take so much larger a share than (say) Paul in the edification of the early Church? The facts, if so, have not come down to us. Besides, the whole point of designating a representative, as outlined above, would be to ensure that this representation should be permanent.

Peter went to Rome; the hardiest of Protestant scholars nowadays will hardly deny that. Whether he was "Bishop" of Rome is a question which cannot be answered, because we do not know whether that title was used by the apostles, or may rather be included in the notion of the apostolate. But it is certain that in early times the prominent Churches jealously kept the record of their spiritual pedigrees; and it is certain that every vestige of Christian tradition traces back the pedigree of the Roman bishops to Peter. As far back as we have any record, the fact of apostolic foundation is treated as if it conferred a special dignity on a given See. Does not parity of reasoning demand that the fact of foundation by the Prince of the apostles should confer a still higher dignity on the two Sees of Antioch and Rome? And if the Antiochene bishops conceived that the unique dignity of the apostolic primacy rested with them, why did they never contest the point?

This chapter is already growing beyond its due measure; I must not, then, attempt even a summary of the Patristic texts on the Papacy, as you may see them set forth in any Catholic manual, and very excellently in Adrian Fortescue's "Papacy in the Early Church". It is enough to say that many Protestant scholars have been sufficiently impressed by them to allow that the See of Peter had from the first a primacy, not of jurisdiction, indeed, but of honour. Now, this distinction is not here in point. Whether the primacy was one of honour or of jurisdiction, it is a central fact in the traditions of the Church; a party out of Communion with the diocese of Rome was ipso facto a party without a primate, and therefore, in the event of a grave schism, was recognisably *the wrong party to belong to*.

Dean Milman, in an inspired moment, allowed himself to admire the astuteness of the Roman prelates in having always managed, in all the Church's doctrinal disputes, to come down on the orthodox side. It would have spared him trouble if he had had the ingenuity to reflect that the reason why we call it the orthodox side is because the Roman prelates belonged to it. The Arians have gone down to history as heretics, and their opponents as Catholics, precisely because the Arians took the non-Roman side. The Nestorians, the Eutychians, the Macedonians, the Donatists are described as heretics, precisely because they took the non-Roman side. That is because, up to the sixteenth century, history was written by Roman Catholics. That the "Orthodox" Greeks, and a fortiori the Protestant sects, attach the stigma of "heresy" to these early theological views is simply a survival—a survival of the Roman Catholic language which their forefathers had used before they, too, went into schism. What the Greek dioceses did in the later Middle Ages, what the Protestants did in the sixteenth century, was precisely what the Arians and Nestorians had done before them; they took the non-Roman side in a dispute. And the stigma of heresy which "Orthodox" Greeks or Protestants attach to Arius and Nestorius comes badly from them. They are tarred with the same brush.

Once you have established the Unity of the Church, the other "notes" of it follow automatically. It is a specific property of the One Church to be the one Church which has never ceased to believe in the permanent possibility of miracles—the note of Holiness. It is the essence of the One Church to be (at least in ambition) world-wide—the note of Catholicity. It is the differentia of the One Church to be in full Communion with the Bishop of Rome—the note of Apostolicity. If you are looking for *a* Church, you will find churches in plenty. If you are looking for *the* Church, you will only find one; for only one contains, as the Church in all ages has contained, a successor of Peter. What need to distinguish whether the primacy due to him be one of honour or of jurisdiction? You have denied him both the one primacy and the other, when you made shipwreck concerning the faith.

XII

The Object and the Act of Faith

We can now elucidate the argument by returning to a metaphor which I used in my second chapter. This is the point at which the inquirer has waded out to sea until he is nearly out of his depth; it remains for him to swim. And by swimming, I mean that he should no longer rest his arguments upon his unaided reason, but allow himself to be buoyed up, henceforward, by the stream of Catholic tradition; in other words, that he should begin to accept doctrines on the authority of the Church.

So far, my contention has been that the credentials of the Church rest upon a certainty which, when viewed with an unprejudiced mind, excludes reasonable doubt. We have argued, first of all, that God is revealed in Nature, then that he is revealed in Christ, and finally that Christ is revealed in his Church, the Catholic Church. This general outline of certainty is sufficient to make us (if we wish to do God's will) take the Church, the revelation of Christ, who is the Revelation of God, for our guide on the rest of our journey; to let her teach us, knowing that her teaching must be his. The further doctrines which she proposes to us she does, indeed, offer to prove; but she does not offer, and could not offer, to prove them (like the contentions already established) on merely philosophical and historical grounds. For their subject-matter is, in great part, altogether outside the reach of the human reason; we believe in them because they have been revealed to us, although we could not have found them out for ourselves.

Thus, the Church invites us to believe in the existence of God and in his Omnipotence on grounds of ordinary human reason. But when she propounds to us the doctrine that there are three Persons in the Unity of this Godhead, she invites us to believe it on her authority, because it has been revealed to her; human reason would never have led us to any conclusion of the kind. Similarly, she invites us to admit our Lord's authority on historical grounds. But when she has to teach us about the doctrine of his Incarnation; when she tells us that in his single Person two Natures were united, a Human Nature and a Divine, she does not mean that any merely historical evidence would have given us ground for so mysterious an inference. She asks us to believe it on her authority, because it has been revealed to her. Again, when she treats the Gospel narratives and the other documents of the New Testament as historically true in their general outline, she bases this confidence on the ordinary canons of historical criticism. But when she affirms that both the Old and the New Testaments are inspired, she invites us to believe that on her authority, because it has been revealed to her. Obviously it would be impossible, at this distance of time, to verify every single statement in the Bible; she can only affirm such a doctrine, then, on grounds of revelation.

This last instance is worthy of particular attention, because the statement that the Bible is an inspired guide to religious truth involves the truth of all the religious teaching which it contains. The Bible is thus one of the great sources of religious certitude; tradition is the other. By tradition we mean that oral teaching which our Lord gave to his apostles, and they in their turn handed on to subsequent generations. If no Christian had ever put pen to paper, there would have still been a stream of oral tradition which would have reached right down to our own day. In course of time, since Christians *have* put pen to paper, the whole of this tradition has by now appeared in written form, like the outcrop, here and there, of some hidden vein of metal. We do not pretend that there is somewhere (locked up at Rome, presumably) a whole deposit of tradition which has never yet seen the light of day. But we do contend that you cannot expect every single element of that tradition to appear in written form among the scarce literary relics that have come down to us from the first two centuries. A belief may happen to be old without happening to have been written down in the very earliest times, especially since we know that there was in the early Church a *disciplina arcani*, a system by which Sacramental doctrine was expounded, not to all comers, but only to those who were actually under instruction. And we do also contend that a doctrine which is "late" in the sense that (say) St. John Damascene was the first author who put it on paper in a distinct form, may yet be part of the primitive tradition.

In such a case as this, we believe in the principle that *melior est conditio possidentis*, "Possession is nine-tenths of the law." If one of the Fathers, even as late as St. John Damascene, confidently affirms, for example, the doctrine of our Lady's Assumption, declaring that he believes it to be the tradition of the Church, that doctrine is "in possession"; those who assail it, not those who assert it, must establish their case; the onus of proof lies with them. If it could be shown that in very early times a monument at Ephesus was pointed out as our Lady's tomb, with the intimation that her body still rested there; or, still better, if it could be proved that any personal relic of our Lady had ever been venerated with the sanction of the Church, then there would be a conflict of tradition, and the matter would remain in doubt. But if there is no such contrary tradition; if the statement was made without fear of contradiction, and no contradiction was ever forthcoming; if the legend does not conflict with any known theological principle—then, we maintain that the presumption is in favour of such a doctrine being true.

And if anybody, upon reading so far, is inclined to throw down this book with the impatient exclamation that "Catholics will believe anything", let him remember that there is a quite considerable literature of apocryphal "Gospels" and "Acts", some of them dating back at least to the second century; these documents were never accepted by the Church, and the incidents they record, often edifying enough, and calculated to promote Catholic piety, have never passed into the continuous tradition of the Church. There is credulity among Catholics, as there is amongst other people; and with Catholics this credulity is apt to take the form of believing in miraculous stories, because Catholics do not reject miraculous stories as such. But there is a very long step between a pious belief which has carried weight with a few thousands of simple souls, and a belief which is sufficiently imbedded in the structure of Christian tradition to be quoted, by a learned and responsible author, as an accepted fact. It does not appear earlier in literature? But consider what a proportion of earlier literature has perished. Oral tradition is untrustworthy? We think so, because we live in an age when everybody reads and derives his knowledge from reading; in more primitive circumstances memory is more tenacious. I have been assured by a very competent informant that round Glastonbury, till quite recently, there was an oral tradition about the old monks which still held its ground. If you talked to the farmers, you would hear nothing but the old Protestant calumnies; if you talked to labourers who could hardly read, you would learn that the old monks were good fellows, and it was a shame when they were turned out.

But (it may be urged) granted that this stream of tradition which you describe has not been enriched by positive invention, at least you will admit that the doctrines which it includes have *developed* with the lapse of time? Thus, for example, the very earliest of the patristic writers show a belief in the Unity of the Divine Nature, and at the same time will assert or imply the Divinity of the Father, of the Son, and of the Holy Ghost; but it was not till later that the Church (doubtless under the inspiration of the Holy Spirit) evolved the doctrine of three Persons and one Substance. Similarly, they believed fully in our Lord's Godhead, and also in his Manhood, but the doctrine of the Hypostatic Union was, once more, a later inspiration. Again, they believed in the reality of our Lord's Presence in the Holy Eucharist, though their senses could tell them that the Sacred Elements were outwardly unchanged, but they held no theory to explain the contradiction; it was only in the Middle Ages that St. Thomas, or some predecessor of his, was inspired to devise the doctrine of Transubstantiation. We do not object (say our critics) to your holding these doctrines as true. But surely you do not propose to hold them as primitive?

This notion of development is one which the Catholic Church refuses to entertain. She may be grateful for the compliment which credits her with inspiration, but she cannot admit it. The Catholic Church is not inspired. She has no mandate to improve upon the deposit of tradition which was entrusted to her at the first. The only "development" to which she will plead guilty is a growing rigidity of doctrinal definition. That is the explanation of the apparent contradiction between this and the preceding paragraph.

As long as no controversy arises, such as is liable to put belief itself in jeopardy, it is enough for the faithful to believe in the Unity of the Godhead, side by side with a belief in the Threefold Invocation; it is enough for them to believe in Christ as God and as Man, without asking how he can be both; it is enough to adore him as present under the Sacred Species, without questioning how it is that this Presence of his eludes the senses. It may even happen that the faithful hold a doctrine of which two rival statements are tolerated (the doctrine of the Sacrifice in the Mass is a case in point). But it happens from time to time that some theologian or theological school, often with good intentions, proposes an explanation of a doctrine which really explains it away. He explains the Trinity by saying that one God assumes three different Functions; or the Incarnation by saying that the Second Person of the Trinity came and dwelt, by some supernatural influence, in one who was personally Man; or that the Presence of Christ belongs, not to the Eucharist itself, but to the soul of the recipient. When such inadequate statements of the faith are proposed, the Church thrusts them out, as a healthy body will thrust out the germs of disease. But she can do so only by defining her traditional doctrine in terms which will make a repetition of the error impossible in future. She does not add to those doctrines; she only protects them against a subtraction. Just as the soles of our feet (for example) become hardened by their own resistance to pressure from without, so at certain points the doctrinal system of the Church develops a rigidity which has been evoked by the attacks of heresy. I do not mean that heresy creates dogma; it is rather the stimulus upon which, in defining dogma, the healthy system of the Church reacts. No (she says to the Sabellian), your statement does not justify the conviction my children have always had; you are making the three Titles of the Godhead impersonal. No (she says to the Nestorian), you are dissociating the Person of Jesus Christ from the Person of the Eternal Word. No (she says to the Receptionist), a change such as you suggest would not affect the substance of the Elements.

I have insisted upon this point, because it would be an obvious cause of additional distrust, calculated to make us ignore the appeal of the Catholic Church altogether, if we had to suppose that the act of submission to her involved drawing a blank cheque (as it were) upon your credulity; declaring your adhesion, not merely to those doctrines which the Church at present holds, but to all those doctrines of which she may contrive to persuade herself in or after your lifetime. You may give in your name to any Protestant denomination with tolerable certainty that your grandchildren will be called upon to believe less, if anything, certainly not more than you. In joining the Catholic Church, you know well enough that the content of the theology which you are embracing can never diminish with time; is it so certain that it cannot increase with time?

It is perfectly true that in matters of devotion the Catholic system admits of, and admits, development. Thus, if a medieval *revenant* should stray into any modern Catholic Church, the chances are that the two statues his eye would first light on would be two statues entirely unfamiliar to him, those of St. Joseph and the Sacred Heart. But the change is one of devotional emphasis, not one of theological assent. And indeed, the whole cultus of the Blessed Sacrament, in the sense of reserving and exposing the Blessed Sacrament for the deliberate purpose of encouraging adoration, is relatively a modern thing. But the doctrine which underlies and justifies that devotion, the doctrine of the Real Presence, is as old as the

Apostolic Fathers, as old as St. Paul himself. The devotional treasury of the Church becomes richer with the centuries; the deposit of faith remains static. Certain doctrines have been more strictly defined; they are thrown into fuller relief, now, against an historical background of old errors. But the doctrine is the same; nor does the Immaculate Conception decree assert any other truth than that which St. Irenaeus asserted in the second century, when he described our Blessed Lady as the antitype and the Advocate of Eve, her first mother.

Meanwhile, if you want to assure yourself that the Catholic Church persists unaltered, you have only to glance at the Catholic type. Where you see men, in the old world or in the new, full of the conviction that there is one visible Church, and that separation from it is spiritual death; where you see men, in the old world or in the new, determined to preserve intact those traditions of truth which they have received from the forefathers, and suspicious of any theological statement which has even the appearance of whittling them away; where you see men distrustful of the age they live in, knowing that change has a Siren voice, and the latest song is ever the most readily sung; where you see men ready to hail God's Power in miracle, to bow before mysteries which they cannot explain, and to view this world as a very little thing in comparison with eternity; where you see men living by very high standards of Christian ambition, yet infinitely patient with the shortcomings of those who fall below it—there you have the Catholic type. It has not changed, and you will find it without difficulty today.

The Church, then, proposes to the inquirer a series of dogmatic truths, her immemorial beliefs; she asks him to accept them on her authority, as the accredited representative of a Divine Teacher. These truths have not all been made the subject of ecclesiastical definition. For instance, no Pope or council has ever pronounced a formal definition as to the existence of the Holy Angels. Yet belief in it is necessary to the Catholic religion; a variety of considerations proves the fact. (1) The existence of the Angels is clearly alluded to in the Bible; it is, therefore, a matter of "divine faith". (2) It is taken for granted in certain ecclesiastical definitions, e.g., by the Fourth Council of the Lateran. (3) The devotional language of the Church everywhere assumes it. (4) It is guaranteed to us by the unanimous consent of the Fathers. Thus Catholic theology forms a whole system of beliefs, not all prescribed to us by the same canon of certainty, but all alike guaranteed to us by the authority of the Church. The inquirer must familiarise himself with the outlines of it before he is received; a bird's-eye view of it will be given in the next chapter but one.

Intellectually speaking, the position of one who "submits to the Church" is that of one who has reached a satisfactory induction—namely, that the Church is infallibly guided into all truth—and can infer from it, by a simple process of deduction, the truth of the various doctrines which she teaches. He does not measure the veracity of the Church by the plausibility of her tenets; he measures the plausibility of her tenets by the conviction he has already formed of her veracity. Thus, and thus only can the human intellect reasonably accept statements which (although they cannot be disproved) cannot be proved by human reason alone.

Is the act of faith, then, nothing more than an intellectual process? Is it merely analogous to the intellectual recognition which a man might give (say) to the law of gravitation, and consequently to all the scientific corollaries deducible therefrom? The analogy falls short of exactness in two ways. The act of faith means something more than this, whether you view it from the psychological or from the theological angle.

As a matter of common-sense psychology, it is evident that a practical step does not follow as the inevitable result of an intellectual conviction; "thought by itself", says the Philosopher, "moves nothing." Just as a man can be convinced of moral principles, convinced, too, that the conduct which he contemplates is worthless, and yet act against the dictates of his reason under the influence of his passions, so, in spite of intellectual conviction, a man can shrink from a practical step out of the mere *vis inertiæ* which is (some of us find) stronger than passion itself. However paradoxical it may seem, it does need a resolution of the will to put the verdict of the intellect into execution. Mere brainwork will not bludgeon you into changing your creed; especially since such a change of creed involves practical consequences—the submission to a ceremony, the adoption of new devotional habits, strained relations with your family or your old friends, and so on. Nothing is more certain as a matter of experience (I appeal with confidence to that of all adult converts) than that a voluntary step is still needed *after* you have become intellectually convinced that Catholicism is true. Perhaps "pulling yourself together" comes as near as may be to a just description of it. For this reason the Church, while insisting (against the Protestants) that the act of faith is seated in the intellect, teaches us nevertheless that this act is directed by the will.

And, theologically speaking, something far more sensational, something far more decisive has happened when a soul is brought into the Church by baptism or by reconciliation. This momentum just alluded to, on its human side an act of the will, on its divine side means the infusion of a supernatural grace, the grace of faith. And, with this infusion, the habit of faith begins here and now for the newly-baptised, is resumed here and now by the newly-reconciled. The water of conviction is changed into the wine of faith. Without altering your logic, this habit transforms the nature of your certitude. It is, if I may use a banal illustration, like the process of tightening a tennis-net—the strain grows more and more intense until at last, suddenly, the tongue slips into its notch. I am fully aware that what I am now saying will sound mere mythology to the outside critic. But, convinced as I am by the Church's teaching (I will not speak of "experience" here) that the act of faith is in truth supernatural, it would be poor loyalty, and poor gratitude, if I omitted to make the unpalatable recognition.

I cannot, however, too strongly insist that this act of faith is not something designed to fill in a gap in the chain of logical argument—that doctrine is Protestantism. Neither the moral effort which submission to the Church involves, nor the grace which is the supernatural coefficient of that effort, carries your reason beyond your premises. You do not, in becoming a Catholic, commit "intellectual suicide"; you follow your reason to its legitimate conclusions. And, if something higher than reason itself supervenes, that is no break in the process. It is not like the suicide of an Empedocles; rather it is like the translation of Enoch, when he "was seen no more, because God took him".

XIII

The Air Catholics Breathe

In this and the following chapters I may be accused of, and must plead guilty to, the use of metaphor. It is impossible to dispense with metaphor in attempting to expound, or even to imagine, the conditions of a supernatural world. But it is to be observed that a thing may be objectively real although it has to be described metaphorically. We are apt to associate the use of metaphor with unreality; to assume that it says more than it means. Thus, if we speak of an orator as having "fire" in his delivery, or describe British seamen as having "hearts" of "oak", we are using the name of a substance to represent the name of a quality; we derive from something concrete, "fire" and "oak", a metaphor for something abstract, "vigour" and "hardiness". In such language the metaphor has an air of unreality; but this is not true of all metaphor. At the risk of being hackneyed, let us recur to the immortal statement of the blind man when they tried to explain what scarlet was like, "I think I understand; it must be something like the sound of a trumpet." A sound and a colour belong to the same order of reality; yet it was only by a metaphor based on his experience of sound that the blind man could entertain the very notion of colour. Similarly, in speaking of the supernatural world, we use metaphorical language about "life", "food", "health", and so on; but in doing so we do not suggest that the supernatural world has less of reality than ours; rather, it has more. We use metaphor, because our faculty of conception cannot really go beyond the terms of our own experience.

I must be understood, then, as meaning what I say, although the poverty of human conception forces me to employ metaphor in doing so, when I say that the Catholic lives with two lives simultaneously, a natural life and a supernatural "life". As birth has brought him into a natural order, so baptism has brought him into a supernatural order of existence. This statement, indeed, does not apply to all Catholics, or only to Catholics. Not to all Catholics here and now; for mortal sin committed after baptism interrupts and paralyses the supernatural life. Not only to Catholics, for (as we shall see in Chapter 18) a non-Catholic Christian who is "in good faith" is a Catholic *malgré lui*. But the normal position of a baptised person is to be a Catholic, and the normal position of a Catholic is to be in a state of grace. And the significance of this supernatural life which the Catholic enjoys is so transcendently superior, that St. Paul does not hesitate to speak of the baptised as already dead to the world of sense and experience. In baptism, they have been mystically buried in the Tomb of Christ, and have risen again with him. "You are dead, and your life is hidden with Christ in God."

Thus, when we speak of "a future life", the phrase is inexplicit. Our life in heaven or in purgatory will be that same supernatural life which we enjoy here and now, lived under different conditions. The common notion of the Protestant-bred Englishman is that the supernatural world, if it exists, is something with which he, at any rate, has no contact until after death—perhaps not till after a general Resurrection.

Something there is, he is assured, called grace, which is mysteriously smuggled into the natural world as you might introduce food into a prison. And there is an outlet as well as an inlet; his prayers, somehow, find their way through and are duly registered; but that is all. To the Catholic mind the supernatural world is, characteristically and predominantly, something which even now intersects and impregnates the world of sense.

Faith, to the Protestant, is primarily a disposition of the affections; a conscious confidence in a Personality. Faith, to the Catholic, has primarily a more general hearing; if grace is the air which the supernatural world breathes, faith is the light in which it is seen. Faith, as under the Old Dispensation, is "the substance of things to be hoped for, the evidence of things which appear not". It was the quality which enabled the patriarchs to serve God in return for a promise which was not to be fulfilled in any lifetime of theirs. Under the New Dispensation, it has the same function, only with this difference—that for us the fulfilment of the promises is not future only, but present. "You are to come to Mount Sion, and to the city of the living God, the heavenly Jerusalem, and to the company of many thousands of angels"—the supernatural world is already with us.

> Does the fish soar to find the ocean,
>   The eagle plunge to find the air,
> That we ask of the stars in motion
>   If they have rumour of thee there?
>
> Not where the wheeling systems darken,
>   And our benumbed conceiving soars,
> The drift of pinions, would we hearken,
>   Beats at our own clay-shuttered doors.

> The angels keep their ancient places;
>   Turn but a stone, and start a wing:
> 'Tis ye, 'tis your estrangèd faces
>   That miss the many-splendoured thing.

There is no touch of pantheism in all this; the two worlds are perfectly distinct, but they intersect.

I do not mean that Catholics (in the vulgar phrase) "see things". The gift of faith is sharply divided from those alleged psychic gifts by which some people suppose that they achieve contact with a different world. For the mystical experiences of the saints are admittedly abnormal; the ordinary Catholic neither has nor expects to have any sensible evidence of that other life which is his. The psychic gift experiences it knows not what; faith knows what it does not experience. It is a conviction, not a consciousness, that the other world is close at hand. And from this conviction flows an attitude of familiarity with the other world which you can trace, amongst Catholics, at two curiously different levels. You can trace it amongst the saints, or those Catholics who are very spiritually minded without being saints. And you can trace it amongst commonplace, casual, lukewarm Catholics. The intersection takes place (you may say) at two different points.

If you read the story of St. Thérèse of Lisieux, who was marked out, during her lifetime, by very few of those celestial favours which (as we believe) have been granted to other perfectly mortified souls, you cannot but be impressed by the extraordinary preoccupation of her mind with eternal values. From her infancy, when she prayed that her mother might die and so attain the joys of heaven, down to her last illness, when she greeted every symptom of her disease with delight, as a step towards her own consummation, she treated death as if it were the mere lifting of a veil. (You will find the same expressions, of course, in St. Paul.) And meanwhile every act and every suffering of her life is seen always in its relation to eternity; the slightest rebuff or mortification is so much "vinegar in the salad"—the whole values of life seem to be inverted, and yet there is nothing strained, nothing forced, nothing unnatural about the terms in which the autobiography describes her feelings. The supernatural has become a second nature to her. Nor is it only by lifelong cultivation that this attitude of familiarity with the other world is produced; you will find it also in the accounts of martyrdom—it was one of the Elizabethan martyrs, I think, who looked forward on the scaffold to a bitter dinner, but a pleasant supper, and the similar attitude of St. Thomas More is notorious history. In all this there is the same instinct of familiarity, which takes the transition from one world to another as a matter of course.

There is among Catholic saints a familiarity which seems to raise this world to the level of eternity. There is among Catholic sinners a familiarity which seems (to non-Catholic eyes) to degrade eternity to the level of this world. The point is most clearly demonstrated in connection with that attitude towards religious things which we call "reverence". For good or for evil, the ordinary, easy-going Catholic pays far less tribute to this sentiment than a Protestant, or even an agnostic brought up in the atmosphere of Protestantism. No traveller fails to be struck, and perhaps shocked, by the "irreverence" or "naturalness" (call it which you will) that marks the behaviour of Catholic children wandering about in church. Even grown-up Catholics will usually talk in church, if anything needs to be said, while Protestants will usually whisper. Those who have read the statement of his beliefs made by my friend, Mr. Julian Huxley, will realise that he is not an exponent of orthodox Christianity. Yet I can recall—I am sure he will not mind my recalling it—his attitude of pained surprise when a

Belgian friend of ours knelt down in a pew to pose for a photograph. I am passing no criticisms, one way or the other, in this matter of reverence; I am simply trying to put on record a difference of attitude. It is perhaps most succinctly stated when it is pointed out that in Catholic books of devotion Almighty God is sometimes addressed not as "Thou" but as "You". And the root of the difference is that the Catholic takes the truths of his religion for granted, however little he lives up to them, whereas the non-Catholic unconsciously behaves as if there were a spell which would be broken if he treated his religion with familiarity; he might wake up suddenly, and find himself alone.

I have said that this supernatural world of which the Catholic has the freedom by right of baptism, here and now, not only intersects our world of sense, but impregnates it. I mean that, for the Catholic, certain merely natural objects are, in various degrees, hallowed by the fact of their association with the supernatural. I say "certain objects"; there is a nature-mysticism which would attach a vague "numinous" influence to all natural objects whatsoever; this at best is poetry, at its worst is pantheism; in any case it is not specifically Catholic. The Catholic view is indeed opposed to this in the same sense in which nationalism is opposed to cosmopolitanism; i.e., the Catholic view singles out certain natural objects here and there as possessing a supernatural significance which the others do not. Let me explain and itemise a little.

The Holy Land in a special way, and in a lesser degree all those places in which saints have lived or died, and in which visions have been seen, acquire this kind of sanctity. The relics of those mortal bodies in which the saints have lived, the instruments of their martyrdom, and even to a less extent such objects as have been in contact with them, clothes, documents, etc., acquire it too. Some breath of it attaches to those common objects, candles, palms, ashes, etc., which have been blessed by the hands of a priest. For the priest's hands are, as it were, repositories of blessing. Watch a Catholic ordination service, and you will see that the priest is being dedicated to God not only in soul but in body, not only as a man but as a thing. When the ordinands lie prone and motionless during the Litanies, you would take them for inanimate objects. When their hands are anointed and bound, you will realise that the Church claims (as it were) those hands for her own. Those hands, newly anointed, are to be kissed by the faithful after the ceremony. The priest, in fact, corresponds in a sense to Aristotle's definition of a slave—he has become a living tool. His personality has become merged in his office. This is, of course, the foundation of all that reverence, sometimes even exaggerated, which pious Catholics show towards the priesthood. In the relic of a saint, in the scene of a martyrdom, in the priest's consecrated hands, they catch an echo of the supernatural.

Is this superstition? Of course, the "question-begging name" has been frequently applied to it. I do not hope to persuade here the uncompromising Englishman who roundly condemns all the Sacramentals of the Church as hocus-pocus, yet "kisses the Book" willingly enough when the law demands that he should do so. But, if any reader be more disposed to consider what is the meaning of this term "superstition", I would suggest that the two elements which make it contemptible to the reason are (1) its arbitrariness and (2) its notion that spiritual influences can actually be *inherent* in outward forms or in material objects. Thus, it offends the reason (in some of us at any rate) to suppose that the seventh son of a seventh son is gifted with any magical powers, or that thirteen is more unlucky than its neighbouring numbers. Nothing but an empirical test, based on accurate statistics, would silence our indignant *Why*? And again, what virtue can there be in the mere attachment of a mascot, in the mere touch of a gold coin, to save you from a motor-accident or to cure you of a sore eye? Reason is affronted because the effect in this case exceeds the cause.

It hardly needs to be pointed out that our Catholic "superstitions" are guiltless on the former count. We do not pretend that there is anything intrinsically "lucky" in the shape or colour of a scapular, in the leaf of the palm as opposed to any other leaf (box, indeed, can be substituted), and so on. The choice of *material* in our Sacramentals is frankly dictated either by convenience or by symbolism.

And, for the second count, it is to be considered that the efficacy which our theology attributes to this or that ceremony, this or that kind of contact with material things, is not a direct efficacy, as if the ceremony or the thing touched exercised any influence *in its own right*. We kiss the priest's hands because the bishop who ordained him, in the name of the whole Church, has prayed Almighty God to bless whatever these hands touch in benediction. We take holy water because this same priest, in the name of the whole Church, has prayed that God would protect in certain ways all those who, out of piety, should so make use of it. In a word, we are treating material objects and vocal formulas as the occasions upon which God himself will see fit to bestow a blessing upon us, in answer to the prayers offered when the object was hallowed, or the formula instituted. An exception must, of course, be made in favour of spots which are kept sacred by historical memories, or of relics which belonged to the saints; here our appeal for help is grounded, not upon the places themselves but upon the events which happened there, not upon the relics themselves but on the merits of the saints who have left them to us. And if, here and there, a taint of superstition (properly so called) infects the devotion of ill-instructed souls, the Church will rather smile at their folly than hold up reproving hands; she knows how to deal with children.

What I have been trying to bring out in this chapter allusively, I fear, and unsystematically—is that Catholics "find themselves" in this world, fit into its scheme of things, precisely because they are convinced (through faith, not through any conscious experience) of the proximity of another world which is equally real to them. And, lest the world of sense should triumph too easily over their imaginations, they bend it to their own will, singling out a scene here, an object there, an action there, to wear the colours of the supernatural and remind them of their home; as a soldier will call his trench "Piccadilly", or a shipwrecked mariner welcome, in his unfamiliar landscape, some memory of the things he loved.

XIV

The Truths Catholics Hold

In this chapter I shall attempt no more than to give some outline of the main truths which Catholics believe as revealed truths. We could not have found them out for ourselves, by the unaided exercise of human reason; we believe them on the authority of Christ revealing; that is, because the Church to which he has bequeathed his teaching office gives us warrant for their assertion.

We believe, then, that within the Unity of the Godhead there is a distinction of three Persons. The Eternal Father, himself the Fount of all being, is the First of these Persons. And we are taught to think of him as begetting, by an act of generation which lies altogether outside of time, a Son equal in glory with himself; or, if you will (so little justice can we do to such a mystery by any conceiving of ours), you may say that he gave utterance to a Word, the express Image of himself, a Word Timeless, Uncreated, Personal. And from these two Persons, Father and Son, proceeds a third Person, the Holy Spirit; the Love of the Father for the Son, the Love of the Son for the Father, is Personal too, and thus the Trinity is completed. The language in which this doctrine is defined does not (as far as we know) come down to us from our Lord himself; but it is the only language capable of safeguarding the beliefs of the earliest Christianity, as it expresses itself both within and outside of the sacred documents. The distinction between the Father, the Son, and the Holy Ghost would be unreal if it were less than Personal; their Unity would be unreal if it were less than substantial.

That anything should exist besides the Blessed Trinity is necessary neither to the Existence nor to the Happiness of the Godhead. But by a voluntary act God has (we can see for ourselves) brought a Creation into existence. We can see, or infer from what we see, parts at any rate of his material creation. But, since we know from the experience of our own soul-life that matter is not everything, it would be a ridiculously parochial assumption to suppose that there was not a vast invisible Creation as well—to suppose that our spirits are the only spirits which exist, God excepted. And in fact, revelation assures us that angelic Beings, pure spirits not united to any material body, do exist—in what number, we have no means of imagining. Some of these spirits, by wilful rebellion against that service of God which was the purpose of their existence, have become confirmed in evil and merited God's eternal reprobation.

We now proceed to a doctrine which is the most paradoxical, perhaps the most improbable, in the whole of theology. It happens, however, to be a matter of daily experience. I mean the fact that God created a being in whom an immaterial spirit was united with a material body; a being, therefore, who should occupy a unique position of liaison between the two halves of Creation. The industrious quarrying of geologists has not made it clear whether there were once creatures, now extinct, which, without being human, approximated more nearly to our type than any of the brutes at present known to us. Still less have they produced any reason for supposing that the human race, as we now know it, is not a single species, but arose independently in various parts of the globe. The probabilities would in any case be against such an assumption. Revelation assures us that the whole human race is, as a matter of fact, descended from a single pair. It also tells us—what science could never prove, what our moral experience might suggest, but could never demonstrate—that this pair were created with natural gifts, and were endowed with supernatural graces, which they never bequeathed to their descendants. They were created (for example) in a state of innocence, their consciences not troubled by those suggestions of evil which now assail us. But a single fault, only less inexcusable than the fault of the rebel angels, reversed the destiny allotted to them and to their posterity. The supernatural endowments, once abused, were withdrawn thenceforward; and even our natural powers were mysteriously hampered by that duality of purpose which is our daily and humiliating experience.

The hope of eternal life was not denied to fallen man, but it was offered, now, only as the prize of a severe probation. And he must struggle against an internal enemy he found too strong for him, with only such crumbs of uncovenanted assistance as God's mercy might afford. It was not intended, in God's Providence, that this pitiful condition of things should endure as long as the world lasted. Man's fault had been foreseen, and with the fault the Remedy. God became Man in order that, dying, he might atone for our sins, and win us the graces normally necessary to the attainment of salvation.

The coming of our Lord was thus not merely a Revelation to illuminate our minds; it was also designed to rescue man from his impoverishment and his spiritual dangers. It was to win for us, not only those "actual" graces by which, since then as before, God has turned our hearts to himself, but "habitual" grace, the state of "justification", in which we are assured of God's friendship, are enabled, during our lifetime, to perform actions pleasing to him, and at our death, if we have persevered, to attain the felicity of heaven. To achieve such blessings for us, it was needful to make amends for the affront offered by the sin of our first parents to the outraged Justice of Almighty God. Although he could have accepted some lesser sacrifice, he determined to make atonement for us himself, and to make it in full measure by the perfect offering of Death.

The Second Person, then, of the Blessed Trinity became Man for our sakes. Without losing or laying aside the Divine Nature which is his by right, he united to his own Divine Person a second, human Nature, in which he was born, lived on earth, and died. Once more the stubborn tradition of the Church could not rest content until it had fortified itself within these safeguards of definition. To think of our Lord's Divine Nature as being annihilated, even temporarily, would be nonsense. A mere limitation of it, if that were thinkable, would not make it become truly human. To deny the reality of the human Nature would be false to all our evidence. Nothing less than a personal identity between the Eternal Word and Jesus of Nazareth would constitute a Divine Witness, or a Divine Victim. Every possible substitute for the received doctrine has been tried, and found wanting.

We believe that the circumstances of our Lord's coming into the world were marked by two miracles especially. In the first place, that she who was to be his Mother was endowed with that same gift of innocence which had been possessed and lost by our first parents; and that this freedom from the curse and the taint of "original sin" was bestowed upon her in the first instant of her Conception.[1] And we also believe that both in and after the Birth of our Lord she remained a pure Virgin. From her, nevertheless, our Lord took a true human Body, which was the receptacle of a true human Soul. And in this human Nature he lived and died and rose again; and at last ascended into heaven, where it still persists.

So much for his natural Body; he has also, as we believe, a supernatural Body, his Church. I am using metaphor here, in the sense which I explained at the beginning of the last chapter. In an ordinary way, when we speak of a collection of people as a "body" of people, we are using an unreal metaphor; we are speaking of a merely abstract solidarity as if it were a concrete thing. But when we speak of the Church as a supernatural Body, although we are still using metaphor, it is not an unreal metaphor; we mean that there is a real, not simply an ideal, solidarity between Christian people in virtue of their "incorporation" into Jesus Christ; and this metaphor of a "body" is the closest, the most apposite we can find. Thus the Church is not merely an institution outside ourselves or above ourselves; it is ourselves. We all know how the Englishman will rally to the appeal of his "country"; how he will lock his doors and hide his ledgers at the very mention of "the State". His prejudice against the Church is partly due to the impression that "the Church" is the spiritual analogue of "the State"; he thinks of it as a tyrannous, prying institution which is bent upon circumscribing his liberty. He does not reflect that "the Church" is also the analogue of a nation or country, but with a supernatural solidarity of its own which far transcends all merely racial ties. In this sublime creation of

[1] It is perhaps worth observing that the doctrine of the Immaculate Conception means this and nothing else. On no subject is Protestant ignorance more inventive; Mr. Shaw, for example, in the preface of "Back to Methuselah", gravely credits us with the notion that our Lady was born of a virgin and not only she, but all her ancestresses.

Providence, all that natural instinct of gregariousness which has given birth to the clan, the tribe, the nation, the party, the club, is pressed into a higher service and acquires a supernatural character. The Church is our Mother, in that her baptism gave us supernatural life; our Mistress, in that her teaching secures us from speculative error; but she is more than that: she is ourselves.

The life of grace which we live in the Church is engendered, nourished, and perfected in us by means of the Sacraments. I shall speak more of these in a later chapter; I only wish to indicate now what is the Catholic doctrine about their general character. I said in my last chapter, speaking of the "sacramentals" (holy water, blessed medals, etc.), that we regard these not as conveying grace in their own right, but as the occasions upon which God will see fit to accord us special graces, in answer to the prayers of his Church. Must we give the same account of the Sacraments themselves? If we do, we lessen their dignity; if we claim more for them, do we not lay ourselves open to the charge of "magic" which the rationalist levels at us?

We answer,[2] that the Sacraments themselves, with one noteworthy exception, do not "convey" grace in the sense in which a boat "conveys" its passengers, but in the sense in which a letter "conveys" information. The lines traced upon the paper do "convey" information, assuming the operation of the reader's intelligence. So the Sacraments "convey" grace, assuming that operation of Divine Power of which they are the covenanted instruments. I say the covenanted instruments; for here we do not merely trust that God will bestow grace in answer to the prayers of his Church; we know that God will bestow grace in fidelity to his own promises. As surely as God

---

[2] I am giving here one theological view, which is not the only view possible to Catholics.

animates with a soul every child that begins to live, so surely he will implant first grace in every soul which receives baptism.

There is, as I have said, one exceptional Sacrament, the doctrine of which is not to be accounted for so easily. We believe that our Lord's human Body and Blood are actually present in the Host and in the Chalice. The explicitness of his own words has forbidden Catholics, in every age, to regard that Presence as conditioned in any way by the faith of the communicant or the worshipper. To say, or to imply, that the change effected by the words of consecration is only a change of significance is to rob our Lord's own words of their plain force. Yet it is a matter of experience that no change perceptible to the senses, whether of size, shape, colour, or texture is observable in the Sacred Elements. Are we to suppose, then, that our senses here delude us? We cannot willingly associate such deception with any work of God. It follows, then, that the *accidents* (the philosophical description of all that falls within the province of our senses) really remain unchanged. And from that it follows that the substance in which those accidents inhere must have been the thing changed; this is the last stronghold of reality. Transubstantiation is the only doctrine which will secure fidelity to tradition on one side, and the evidence of our senses on the other. The Mass, in which this momentous change is effected, is held by Catholics to be a true Sacrifice—the renewal of that Sacrifice made once for all on Calvary.

And here let it be observed, that the four most baffling mysteries of our religion—the Trinity in Unity, the Union of Natures in the Incarnation, the Real Presence in the Holy Eucharist, and the relation between Grace and Free Will—those four mysteries, over which controversy has been most embittered throughout the centuries, lie there centred where human thought most fails us; they drive in their wedges (so to speak) at the weakest points in our human philosophy. Three Persons in one Substance, two Natures united in one Person—mysterious doctrine, assuredly; but is not the principle of individuation itself a mystery, over which philosophers have wrangled without attaining any measure of agreement? A change of substance which leaves the accidents unaffected—hard for us to imagine; but, then, whose imagination is not puzzled by the whole relation of universals to particulars? Grace all-powerful, yet the human will free—it sounds a paradox; yet is there not paradox already in the reaction of the free human will upon the motives which "determine" it? There is nothing inconceivable in doctrines such as those we have been citing; they are outside our experience, but not repugnant to thought. The imagination, however, naturally recoils from the contemplation of them, because their very terms plunge us into mystery.

I have mentioned the doctrine of actual grace; it would be beyond the scope of my present undertaking to expound the Catholic system, or rather systems, upon the point. It is enough to recall here that there are two notice-boards (as it were) to guide us, two general principles which secure us from misconceptions. On the one side, it is universally admitted, against the Pelagians, that nobody ever goes to heaven except through the free grace of perseverance. On the other side it is universally admitted, against the Calvinists, that nobody ever goes to hell except through his own fault.

The last paragraph reminds us of one department of Catholic theology which needs mention before this rude summary of its teaching is complete—I mean, its doctrine of the Last Things. We believe that the soul is judged immediately after its final separation from the body. If it is found to be outside God's friendship, it is condemned to eternal punishment, and a punishment which does not stop short with mere regrets, mere moral torments. If it is found in a state of grace, it is secure of its passage to heaven. But, for most of us, an expiation still remains to be made; nor do we achieve eternal happiness until we have paid the "debt" of suffering in which our sins, long ago forgiven, have involved us. It is for the lightening of this expiation that we pray when we offer our suffrages for the dead; it is for some remission of this debt, and not for any forgiveness of sins, that we hope when we try to gain an "indulgence". Beyond that lies the open vision of God, and such felicity as we may not dare to imagine. The justice of these, God's dealings, whether in general or in particular, will be fully revealed when this material order of creation ceases, and the bodies which are the connatural companions of our soul-life are restored from their corruption, a new creature in Jesus Christ.

XV

The Rules Catholics Acknowledge

The Church exercises her practical authority in two quite different ways. She acts judicially in interpreting the Divine Law; and, when her decision is given with due formality, she claims the same infallibility in morals as in faith. She acts legislatively in prescribing certain rules for her own children, in matters which are of themselves indifferent. Thus, she acts judicially when she applies the Divine Law against murder by condemning suicide. She says that suicide is wrong for a Jew or for a heathen, as for a Christian. She expects her own children not merely to refrain from committing suicide, but to acknowledge that suicide is wrong. She acts legislatively, when she tells us to abstain from flesh meat on Fridays. She does not suggest that this law binds a Jew or a heathen; she legislates only for her own subjects. Nor does she invite the opinions of her children on the relative value of flesh meat and other meats; she only expects them to obey a rule.

It might seem at first sight that the judicial activity above referred to was unnecessary. For the Divine Law—the Church herself maintains it—is written in man's heart, and ought not to need any external authority for its enforcement; conscience itself ought to be enough for us. But it is painfully observable that disobedience to conscience on the part of a large multitude is apt to produce an erroneous conscience in society at large; it is to inform and to correct this erroneous conscience that the Church, from time to time, has to issue her judicial pronouncements, defining the scope of the Divine Law more precisely.

An obvious instance is the history of duelling. Most of us, in this humanitarian age, would agree that duelling is wrong. We have perhaps forgotten how much the duellist had to say for himself. *Scienti et volenti non fit injuria,* No injustice is done to a man by an action which he knows about and permits; if then A gives B, and B gives A, the right of killing, there is no injustice done. Moreover, the duel had its practical advantages. How much occupation is given to our courts of law by libel actions and actions for divorce! Yet either was unnecessary when a personal grievance could be put to the arbitrament of the sword. There was something to be said for the system; but no sophistry could really conceal the fact that it was against God's law. On the other hand, in an age when men went about armed, it was morally certain that disputants in the heat of passion would exchange blows. And in fact the thing was so common, that this form of disobedience to conscience became an organised institution, with its code and its courtesies. Society in general had, for many centuries, a false conscience on the subject. And occasionally a speculative theologian would advance the opinion that the duel was not murderous. So challenged, from the sixth century to the nineteenth, the Church has always replied with a condemnation.

It is with no pride that a Catholic recalls these facts; it is a melancholy reflection that public opinion can set conscience so long at defiance. I adduce the facts, merely to show that a situation can arise in which the Church must exercise judicial rights if the Divine Law itself is to be made clear to the consciences of her own subjects. Nor has she only the power to bind; she has the power to loose. Worldliness may make men's consciences too lax; an exaggerated pietism may make them too rigid. Is betting wrong? (In itself, I mean; the disasters which may arise from it in practice are too obvious to need recounting.) The bet belongs, in some ways, to the same order of things as the duel; the duellist risks his life, the gambler his fortune. In Protestant England a dogma grew up, which is still a tradition amongst many good people, that betting in itself is wicked. Here the Church refuses to take the strict view. Subject to the claims of his family and other similar claims, a man has a right to venture his money in support of his opinion, though he has not a right to venture his life. There would be great practical advantages gained if the Church could declare that betting and gambling in themselves were contrary to the Divine Law; much misery, doubtless, could be avoided. But, because she is committed to following a just principle of interpretation, the Church will not tie up the consciences of her faithful subjects by a scruple which is unreal.

By claiming to act in this judicial capacity the Church, it seems to me, has a manifest advantage over the other Christianities today. I do not mean that a clear statement of Catholic doctrine will compel obedience, even in a Catholic country (so called). The history of duelling, alluded to above, affords painful evidence of that. For (1) it is morally certain that a command of the Church which is distasteful to Nature or to prejudice will in fact be largely disobeyed by undisciplined souls. (2) In times of national or political excitement, especially, the prevalence of such disloyalty will lead another set of consciences to wonder "whether the Church really cares"; her tenderness towards the erring, her deliberateness in

forming judgments, will be mistaken for a toleration of practices which, on paper, she condemns. Thus a kind of public
opinion may be built up in defiance of the Church's express
decision; priests, even, may be found who will give absolution too readily to the half-repentant. Legislators must not
expect the Church to do their police work for them. She will
not decide in a particular case without laborious accumula-
tion of evidence, and such delay often lets opportunity slip.
She is dealing with human material, without any power of
physical coercion; men's consciences will always be stam-
peded by passion, and their wills are weak.

But, for a soul that really seeks to know the will of God,
there is a consolation hardly to be over-estimated in the
consciousness that the Church offers you guidance, and a
guidance which, at least in its solemn expressions, cannot err.
I have alluded already in my tenth chapter to the embarrassment which Christian teachers already feel, and will (it is to
be feared) feel acutely before long, in the matter of divorce. It
is already possible for a Protestant, loosely attached to his
creed, to be in a serious conflict of mind as to where his true
duty lies in this unhappy business. It is not possible for a
Catholic, even loosely attached to his creed, to feel any doubt
on the question so long as his reason is unclouded by passion.
It is not that his Church tyrannously claims the right of
forbidding to him a freedom allowed to others. He must not
say "My Church forbids it"—that is inaccurate. He must say
"God forbids it, and my Church fortifies me in that belief."
The same difficulty is beginning to arise, the same uncompromising attitude is being adopted by the Church, over that
modern propaganda which would artificialise the use of marriage. Here the hesitation of non-Catholic thought is already
perceptible; the demand of individual minds for a ruling on
the subject is more persistent and more acute; nor is the

situation improved by the fact that modesty disinclines the virtuous from its discussion. The issue is real; in six or seven years time the population should be actually dwindling. For a man of principle, it is everything to be guided authoritatively in such a matter, even though the guidance afforded be unpalatable to his selfish instincts.

No doubt but the strictness of our theology on these two points will produce, is producing, apostasies. The Church which was once accused—by the Montanists, the Donatists, the Reformers, the Jansenists—of making life too easy for its members, is now accused of making life too hard for them. The Church which was once suspected of encouraging men to "do evil in order that good might come", is now at a disadvantage precisely because it refuses to give them such licence. But meanwhile, this very rigidity of hers is attracting those responsible and conscientious minds which are distressed by the moral anarchy of our day. Even if there should be a loss of quantity, there will be a gain in quality. Catholicism appeals, no longer to the antiquarian faddist or to the restless in search of spiritual adventure, but to the lovers of order. It beckons like a life-boat to shipwrecked souls who have seen the conventions go down under their feet.

It will be objected, of course, that this craving for moral guidance is in fact a sign of weakness: a man ought not to need any supernatural sanctions for doing that which his own conscience tells him to be right. But the point is ill taken. Man is still a social animal, and his ethical judgments will not rest themselves contentedly upon a merely individual basis. The true Kantian, who will act in such a way that he could wish his action to be a law for all other men, without any reference to what other men are in fact doing around him, is a rare specimen, and, to tell the truth, is not far removed from a prig. There is a kind of intellectual modesty which makes the Englishman ashamed of "setting up to be better than other people". He will not set out on a solitary tramp for heaven; he will make up a party. So long as the traditions of the society in which he lives are manifestly in accord with the sentiments of natural morality, he will follow them cheerfully, not asking (if he is a Protestant Englishman) any guidance from his spiritual superiors. But when those traditions are themselves assailed, and in connection with matters so vital as birth and marriage, he is in a quandary. His good principles prevent him from falling in with the low standard of morality which prevails around him; his intellectual modesty forbids him to establish and to preach a code for which he alone is responsible. It is not weakness of moral fibre, but fear of intellectual singularity, seen as intellectual superiority, which bids him find, somewhere, a society like-minded with himself.

Lest this analysis of modern hesitations should seem extravagant, let me say that a Catholic priest of my acquaintance was lately decoyed by a comparative stranger into a darkened room at one of the Universities, where a dozen or more undergraduates, to whom he was not introduced, plied him with very intimate questions about sexual morality; the burden of their problem being always "Why shouldn't I?" They were not Catholics; they had no intention, so far as he knows, of becoming Catholics. They wanted to know what a priest would say.

I say, then, that the claim of the Catholic Church to infallible guidance in questions of morals is likely to attract even while it repels; not precisely because it is infallible, but because it is responsible, accredited guidance. On the other hand, there is a prevalent feeling that the Church, instead of resting satisfied with this momentous function of hers in interpreting and applying the Divine Law, goes beyond her commission in perplexing the consciences of her members with a multiplicity of mere regulations which are her own. Instead of encouraging them in habits of piety, she will bind them to a weekly attendance at Mass, to a yearly precept of Confession and Communion. Instead of recommending simplicity of living, she will make them abstain from flesh food one day in the week. Instead of interesting them in works of piety, she obliges them in general terms to the support of their spiritual pastors. The result (we are told) is a formalism which is content with a minimum, because a minimum had been prescribed.

Nor is it only by their externality that these rules offend, but by their capriciousness. The inquirer finds, when he begins to study the Church at first hand, that some of the rules over which conflict has raged most fiercely are not and never were rules of the universal Church. The celibacy of the clergy, the denial of the chalice to the laity, which have been such a frequent source of discontent (for example) in Bohemia, are not and never have been applied to those Catholic dioceses in the East which kept their own vernacular rites. Again, the *Ne temere* decree, which is responsible for so many vexed matrimonial cases, was not issued so as to be everywhere in force; nor was the "Index of Forbidden Books", much criticised as an invasion of private liberty. How comes it that a Church which is so proud of its universality will legislate in one way for this nation, in another for that, and expect the faithful observance of legislation, from which a mere change of residence might dispense?

The answer to this latter difficulty is that such regulations belong not to the doctrine but to the discipline of the Church. She does not exist merely as the interpreter of eternal laws which she has no power to change; she has the right, also, of "binding and loosing", of *making* laws for her own subjects, like any secular power. That different disciplinary regulations should be in force at Westminster and Baghdad, under a single Pope, is no more anomalous than that different legal systems should obtain in England and in Scotland. Sometimes there is an immemorial privilege to be consulted; the Eastern "rites", for example, could trace back their traditions to a remote antiquity. Sometimes an exception is made in view of local conditions—to avoid, for example, a conflict with secular authorities which might perplex the loyalty of Catholic citizens. But in such cases the Church does not exceed her powers in making exceptions, for she is herself the legislator. She cannot dissolve the bond of a valid and consummated Christian marriage; that would be to usurp powers not her own. But she can lay down for her own subjects a list of conditions under which marriage is to be celebrated, dissent from which will accordingly invalidate the contract; and here, since the details of legislation are not prescribed by Divine Law, she can, if she will, vary her policy.

We have rules, it is true; and rules will always demoralise certain minds by giving them the impression that they need do no more than what is actually prescribed. But all voluntary associations must have rules, if only as a test of membership; it is only established Churches that can dispense with such a safeguard. Our rules are more subjected to criticism than those of other religious bodies (the Salvation Army, for instance), because obedience to them is a condition of membership in a Society with claims so far-reaching, with sanctions so tremendous. It seems disproportionate that failure to comply with a mere regulation should involve the danger of losing eternal happiness. But the gravamen of the offence lies, not in the importance of the command itself, but in the majesty of the authority which is challenged. It is a poor and a haggling faith that will believe the Church to be infallible when her decision is made upon faith or morals, yet will not render even a bare obedience to her disciplinary requirements.

Obedience, it is true, is more highly rated as a virtue amongst Catholics than amongst Protestants. And yet, is it so certain that Catholics are in the wrong? "Who is so wise as to know all things? . . . If your opinion is good, and you let it go and follow another for the love of God, you will make the more advance." So speaks, not the Council of Trent, but the *Imitation of Christ.*

XVI

The Strength Catholics Receive

"And they bring to him one deaf and dumb, and they besought him that he would lay his hand upon him. And taking him from the multitude apart, he put his fingers into his ears, and spitting, he touched his tongue, and looking up to heaven, he groaned, and said to him, Ephpheta, which is, Be thou opened." Such is the description which one of our earliest records gives of a miracle attributed to our Lord. Whether there is any mystical significance in the fact that this *miraculé* lived, not in Palestine itself but on Phoenician soil, does not concern us here. What is evident is that our Lord, who (according to our records) was capable of performing a miracle by a mere word, and even at a distance from the patient, did, on one occasion at least, go through an elaborate external ceremony to effect the same purpose. He looked up to heaven, as if in invocation; he applied physical touch, and even made use of a material substance in doing so; he pronounced a verbal formula to correspond with the significance of his action. In fact, he made a deliberate display of the sacramental principle, combining with that internal prayer—which surely might have been efficacious by itself—the use of form and matter. He went through the gestures of a physical cure, and made those gestures the vehicle of a miraculous cure. It was an efficacious sign, symbolising what was performed and performing what was symbolised.

It is an old dream of the rationalist theologian, to set about convincing us that there was a time, very early in its history, when the Christian Church did not believe in the sacramental principle. The moderns, in attempting to produce this conviction, attribute the growth of the sacramental idea to the corroding influence of the mystery religions upon Christian thought. For the notion that this contamination took place in the second or even the third century—a notion which has found some favour with controversialists—the scholars have nothing to say. As a matter of scholarship it is quite clear that if such contamination took place, it must have taken place before the books, even the earlier books, of the New Testament were written. So far as baptism and the Holy Eucharist are concerned, the sacramental principle is fully recognised by St. Paul, is fully recognised by the Synoptic Gospels as part of our Lord's teaching. The contention, in fact, is not that Christianity was deformed by the enervating influence of the second century, but that it was deformed by St. Paul.

The theory is wholly unconvincing, because wholly gratuitous. To distinguish between the Christianity of Christ and the Christianity of St. Paul is to invent for yourself an imaginary picture of Christ for which no document lends any sort of authority. The mental process of these critics is the following—Christ was a great Prophet, and his teaching was always on a high spiritual level. But the whole notion that forms of words or physical contact can produce effects upon the soul of man is magical, and therefore on a low spiritual level. There must, therefore, originally have been a "pure doctrine" of Christ in which such conceptions played no part, though it comes down to us, even in its earliest forms, overlaid already with apostolic accretions.

It will easily be seen that such reasoning is wholly a priori; if assumes that the critic is the true judge of what is "high" and what is "low" in the scale of spiritual values, and that our Lord's judgment in the matter must necessarily coincide with his. There is no sort of evidence that this "pure doctrine" ever existed, except in the mind of the critic. The candid atheist might be led by the evidence to suppose that our Lord himself never existed, that "Christ" was a mere cultus-title; or he might be led by the evidence to suppose that our Lord, in spite of the high tone of his general teaching, was nevertheless infected with materialistic, "magical" ideas. He would never be led by the evidence to suppose that there was a Christ whose teaching both St. Paul and the Gospels misrepresent. That is only mythology.

I have said something, in Chapter 13, about the Sacraments in general. It remains to say something about their number and their separate characteristics. That there should be seven Sacraments is in itself, to the unfriendly critic, a suspicious circumstance. We all know that seven is a mystical number; does it not look, then, as if the Church had deliberately marked off seven of her rites and decided, quite arbitrarily, that these should be considered Sacraments, while all other external aids to devotion are only to be called "sacramentals"? This would not be so high-handed a proceeding, if she did not add in the same breath that these seven Sacraments are of our Lord's own institution. For many ages of the Church their enumeration seems to have been a matter of opinion, and to have differed widely; sometimes as many Sacraments as twelve would be mentioned, sometimes as few as two or three; and it is only since Peter Lombard that the orthodox definition has prevailed. If our Lord instituted seven

Sacraments and no more, why was it left for the Middle Ages to discover the fact?

The answer to this difficulty is a very simple one—that the difference in question is a difference, not of doctrine, but of name. *Sacramentum*, the acknowledged equivalent of *mysterion* in Greek, was a word loosely used in the age of the Fathers; it was the schoolmen, with their logical determination to make one word mean one thing, who resolved that it must have a connotation and a denotation of its own. They restricted its use; and if the restriction was arbitrary, that does no harm, for all use of words is arbitrary; they are labels which man makes and attaches to things for his own convenience. That convenience is best served by ensuring that the same label should always attach to the same thing—a principle which, unfortunately, the moderns have not sufficiently grasped. The question, then, is not whether the label "sacramentum" could not be attached to more or less than seven things in the fourth century. The question is whether the things to which Peter Lombard attached the label *sacramentum* were not, in fact, seven things which had always been recognised by the Church as conveying in a unique manner the grace of Christ to men.

And here the Orthodox Churches of the East shed an interesting light on the case. Their traditions had crystallised long before the age of the schoolmen, and during that age their attachment to the Roman See was broken, at least for practical purposes. There was no likelihood, then, that the Greeks should be impressed by Latin definitions; if anything, they would have been likely to repudiate such definitions merely as a fresh proof that the Latins were unprimitive. It was, therefore, independently of the main stream of Latin theology that the Greeks selected seven Sacraments, and selected the same seven. Is it not clear that, although seven rites may only have acquired the exclusive label of "sacraments" in

the twelfth century, the unique importance of those seven
rites was recognised even before the ninth century, in what
Protestants call the "undivided Church"? The fact that they
had as yet no common name to distinguish them from the
other rites of the Church makes the circumstance of their
recognition doubly important. Language may react upon
thought to its confusion; but here thought had preceded
language by at least three centuries.

Catholics believe, then, that our Lord instituted seven Sacraments, or visible signs, which were to signify and to confer
sanctifying grace. Five of these may be regarded as the frame-
work of a life. The child is born, then it is baptised. It reaches
the age of reason, then it is confirmed. At the end of the
journey, Extreme Unction prepares the soul for its last passage. There may come, in between, a solemn moment when
man and woman are joined in matrimony, or when a man is
consecrated to God in the service of his priesthood. These are
special expedients for special emergencies. There remain two
Sacraments which are of frequent repetition—Confession and
Holy Communion. In dealing with each of the seven, I shall
confine myself here to the ungrateful task of considering the
characteristic difficulties which are felt over them, without
enlarging upon their Providential design or the comfort which
our souls derive from them.

Baptism has this characteristic difficulty—that it is bestowed
upon souls, usually, which can make (as far as we can judge)
no intelligent response to the action by which grace is
conferred upon them. This is occasionally true of Extreme
Unction, and of death-bed absolutions; but these cases are
manifestly exceptional; whereas infant baptism is the normal
practice of the Church. It is hard to know whether we should
admire more the logical consistency which has induced the
Baptists and others to defer the christening rite until years of

discretion are reached, or the Providential common-sense which has deterred the other denominations from following their example. Doubtless there are latitudinarians who excuse themselves with the reflection that "at any rate it can do no harm"; but the implication of infant baptism, where its efficacy is really believed, is a doctrine that might well stagger the most robust faith. For there is no question, here, of supposing that the rite produces its effects through any impression which it makes upon the mind; nor yet that it derives its value from any dispositions already existing in the subject—it is naked sacramentalism, this act which professes to awaken a soul to the life of grace through the mere application of an external ceremony.

For Catholics, at any rate, this belief is assured by the authority of the Church. It is a part of her tradition; and we believe it to have been so from the earliest times: when we hear of St. Paul baptising "the household of Stephanas", or that the gaoler at Philippi "himself believed, and his whole house", it is reasonable to assume that there may have been infants involved. But to my own mind, at least, the "argument from prescription", so much questioned by Protestant controversialists, is far the safest guide on the subject. If at any time in the history of the Church, especially in those early ages when baptism was sometimes deliberately deferred until the hour of death, any bishop or any local church had introduced so momentous an innovation as that of baptising an unresponsive subject, incapable of making an intelligent act of faith, must there not have been some protest, some controversy, some schism (even), to mark the change and to assert the primitive tradition?

Confirmation is a rite not explicitly instituted by our Lord in any words which have come down to us. Yet it can be safely assumed that he did enjoin it, since it forms part of the normal procedure employed by the Church of the Apostles. The chief difficulty to be urged in connection with it is this—where it is mentioned in the Acts of the Apostles, the bestowal of the rite seems regularly to be accompanied by outward and quasi-miraculous evidences of its spiritual value. Those on whom the apostles have laid their hands "speak with tongues"—a phrase which, whatever its precise meaning, certainly refers to some kind of prophetic transport. Here, then, we have an instance in which the alleged "prophetic ministry" of the Apostolic Church has passed into the "institutional ministry" of a later Christendom. No outward symptoms, now, attend and attest the gift of the Holy Spirit; are we within our rights, then, in supposing that the Sacrament was *permanently* instituted, and that grace still comes to the recipient? Once more we have to repose our confidence in the Church; it was her conviction, evidently, that the essence of the rite was sacramental, and the miraculous accompaniments only accidental. We believe that Providence saw fit to externalise, in a special way, the effects of this particular grace among the early Christians; yet we ourselves receive, so we trust, the same inward strengthening as they.

Something of the same difficulty arises, though in a more acute form, over the Sacrament of Extreme Unction. An apostolic reference (Jas 5:14)[1] is explicit as to the primitiveness of the rite; but the casual reader of that passage would suppose that a miracle of healing, on the physical plane, was its primary purpose, and its spiritual effects only secondary. Whereas anyone who is conversant with the existing practice of the Church knows that the idea of spiritual medicine is uppermost. Many priests can tell you stories of strange recoveries following upon the administration of this Sacrament and the

[1] "Is any man sick among you? Let him bring in the priests of the church and let them pray over him, anointing him with oil in the name of the Lord."

lifted eyebrows of the doctor next morning; but these physical results are today exceptional. Indeed, so strongly does the Church insist upon the sacramental character of the rite that all her legislation discourages frequent recourse to its use. Has she not, then, taken it upon herself to alter what was once a ministry of healing into a symbol and an alleged vehicle of spiritual effects?

It is to be remembered, however, that the Church has her own notions about the relation of sin to disease. Or rather, they are not her own notions, but his who said to the palsied man, "Thy sins are forgiven thee." It is not that we trace any direct connection between the soul's state and the body's. But we do think of disease, and whatever ills the flesh is heir to, as the punishment of sin, and primarily (though not exclusively) as the punishment in the individual life of sins which the individual has committed. In our view, then, forgiveness of sins could not be a corollary of physical health; physical health is, in this particular case, a corollary of forgiveness. The forgiveness of sins, therefore, although St. James mentions it as if it were an afterthought, is the direct effect, physical health an indirect effect, of the Sacrament.

The two Sacraments which are concerned with entering upon new "states of life"—that is, matrimony and ordination—could hardly be excluded from the list except on pedantic grounds. We recognise, of course, the sacred character of marriage even outside the Christian covenant; and indeed it was a "Sacrament" of the Old Dispensation as it is a Sacrament of the New. But those who compare the legislative tone which our Lord adopts about it (Mark 10:5, etc.) with the highly mystical character attributed to it by St. Paul (Eph 5:28) will hardly doubt that from the first the Church thought of marriage as raised to a different order of things by Christ's command. In all her history, whether she has been assailed by

Gnostics and "Manicheans" who decried marriage, or by rationalists who would weaken its obligation, she has shown no change of front. And that ordination must be sacramental in character is obvious, if the sacramental system as a whole is to be consistently recognised. The stream does not rise higher than its source, nor could a real consecration be expected from an unconsecrated priest.

There remain two Sacraments, distinguished, as I have pointed out, by the frequency of their repetition. They stand on different footings; for, whereas frequent Communion was as characteristic of first-century as of twentieth-century Christendom, easy Confession certainly marks, not indeed a doctrinal, but a disciplinary change of attitude. The criticism urged against our present practice is not so much that auricular confession has outlived public confession (if it has not actually replaced it); rather, what has to be admitted is that the primitive Church was more exacting in its moral attitude than ours; that penances were real and protracted; that the sinner might even be refused absolution until the approach of death made its bestowal urgent. Our discipline has been relaxed; what excuse can we offer to our facile critics for its relaxation?

The answer is twofold. In the first place, a young and persecuted Church must necessarily insist upon a high standard of membership. Its converts may be called upon at any time to attest their faith with their blood; they must be proved, therefore, in a hard school if the honour of the institution is to be maintained. If there is any doubt as to their moral stamina, it is best from every point of view that at first, perhaps for a number of years, they should only be admitted to half-membership as catechumens. And this habit of postponing baptism makes the remission of post-baptismal sin a less urgent problem. I suppose that all Catholic missions in heathen countries are, for this reason, much stricter in their discipline than the Christian community at home. But there is a further reason to explain the "development". St. James writes, "Confess your sins one to another, and pray for one another that you may be saved. For the continual prayer of a just man availeth much." The Church dares to be indulgent to her children precisely because the great mass of prayers offered for her intentions, both on earth and (as she believes) in heaven, forms a reservoir of communicable merit. As the early martyrs were allowed to intercede for those who had apostatised in the persecutions, and so lessen their canonical penance, so the merits of those martyrs and of the other saints, and of all faithful people, are set off by the Church against the demerits of her own weak members, and (so far as her judicial competence extends) allowed to atone for them. Such solidarity is there, according to the Catholic view, in the Christian body.

And if we have altered the practice of our remote predecessors in this respect, let it be observed that we have not altered their principle. The *instinct* of the Catholic Church, in opposition to the sects, has always told in favour of leniency. The notion that post-baptismal sin, or certain forms of post-baptismal sin, could not be forgiven has been the doctrine of the Montanist, the Novatianist, or the Calvinist; successive attempts have been made to foist this rigorist attitude upon the Church, and always they have been repudiated. The Roman bishops have been visibly active in this opposition. It is as if our Lord's words to St. Peter about forgiving his brother "until seventy times seven" had been understood in an official sense, and had formed the mind of his successors in the direction of indulgence.

Our critics accuse us today, as the Tertullianists accused our forefathers, of compromising principle by this laxity. The Church remains unmoved; she shook off Jansenism as she shook off Novatianism. She insists upon one thing—penitence. Her bestowal of forgiveness is conditional upon a disposition in the soul of the penitent, sorrow for sin combined with a purpose (which may or may not prove effectual) of avoiding it in the future. Whether such penitence is truly present, her ministers can only judge by outward manifestations; they have no infallible guidance to read the secrets of the heart. If the penitent has deceived himself and the priest about his own dispositions, the sentence of absolution is inoperative. Beyond that, the Church will have nothing but tenderness for the sinner; she knows that we are dust.

I have written already about the doctrine of the Holy Eucharist; I only want to add a word here about Communion as a Sacrament, as a means of strengthening the soul with supernatural grace. Of its primitiveness, of its sacramental character, there can be no reasonable doubt. But one point is worth raising—has not the practice of the Church in encouraging or failing to encourage frequent Communion differed in different ages? Is it not true that a pious Catholic a century or two ago did not approach the altar much oftener than a lax Catholic of today? What, then, is the teaching of our Church, the permanent tradition of our Church, as to the dispositions required in the communicant, and the value of frequent reception?

The answer is that as frequent Confession is a disciplinary, frequent Communion is a devotional development. Or rather, it is not a development; it is the persistence of an instinct. It was taken for granted while the Church was still small and compact. The Church grew, and became scattered; priests were few, and persecution made assemblies dangerous; perforce Christians had to be content with occasional churchgoing. When the persecutions were at an end, charity had begun to grow cold; Chrysostom and Augustine and other Fathers tried to restore a public opinion on the matter, but by now it was too late. The ideal was lost, to reappear, not in the so-called "Ages of Faith" but with the great Saints of the Counter-Reformation. But a fresh obstacle greeted this revival. Jansenism, with its severe ethical theory, infected the Catholic world with a scruple. Only in our own time has frequent Communion been restored to its natural place in devotion—it is like a stream that has long sunk underground, to reappear in the sunlight.

The Church, then, is not only our accredited teacher, not only the "competent authority" which interprets laws and makes rules for us. She is also the custodian of the Seven Sacraments. Here again she must be our interpreter; who shall tell us, for example, what constitutes validity of ordination if not she? Here again she must regulate, according to the needs of the time, for the general good of her subjects. But it is as the dispenser of supernatural graces that she most endears herself; she nourished us at her bosom, and it is she who will close our eyes in death.

XVII

The Ambitions Catholics Honour

In the last three chapters we have been dealing with certain aspects of Catholicism which are integral to, and characteristic of, its system. The profession of certain beliefs on the authority of the Church, obedience to her laws, participation in her Sacraments—these are constitutive elements of the Catholic life as such. But there are certain points of view which do, in fact, distinguish Catholicism from the other Christianities, though there is no reason *in the nature of the case* why this should be so. In particular this description applies to the Catholic notion of asceticism, properly so called; I mean the deliberate abstention from, or at least indifference to, comforts, amenities, pleasures, etc., which are not in themselves sinful, for the love of God. There is no reason in the nature of things why any Protestant should not preach and honour such an attitude. But as a matter of fact they do not, except for a few who are avowedly imitators of our system. Puritanism, with its rigorous black-and-white division of conduct into what is sinful and what is laudable, openly decried all "works of supererogation" as unscriptural. The Protestantism of today, everywhere tinged with rationalism, decries them as superstitious. A Buddhist would probably view the life of a Carmelite nun with more sympathy than a Baptist.

I do not mean to deny that Protestants often live self-sacrificing lives, to a degree that may well make a lax Catholic blush. But, when pressed to explain their behaviour, they will always plead some practical excuse. A simple style of living, they will tell you, enables them to devote more time to their work, more money to the relief of their brethren; abstinence from certain pleasures, which are in themselves legitimate, "sets a good example" to those who would be likely to abuse them, and so on. It is not part of the Evangelical tradition, still less is it part of the rationalist tradition, that there is more "perfection" in a life which uses God's creatures sparingly than in one which uses them to the full. People are in the habit of describing such views as "medieval"—a curious understatement of the case since they were already in vogue as far back (at least) as the fourth century.

There is an Oriental notion that all matter is evil, and that the spiritual life consists in an escape from it. The self-inflicted tortures of the fakir present this idea in its crudest form. And it is commonly assumed that this notion must have insinuated itself during the early centuries, into the Christian Church; that fasting, vigils, flagellations, etc., belong to a corrupt stream of doctrine, from which "the Church" was happily purified at the Reformation. But this view of the facts is very questionable history. What is certain is that the Church, from New Testament days onwards, was continually forced into an attitude of opposition by those Gnostic teachers who "forbade to marry" and commanded "to abstain from meats"; that such doctrines were energetically repudiated by the earlier Fathers, and again by St. Augustine when they reappeared with the Manicheans. Is it likely that, despite this conscious reaction, the Church should have allowed practices to creep into her system which were in fact based on the very theories she was concerned to deny?

Historically, the development of ascetic ideas in Christendom is something quite different. It is plain that the ideal of martyrdom was, from the earliest days of the persecutions, associated in Christian minds with a high degree of sanctity. Then, since many had suffered imprisonment and torture for the name of Christ without being actually put to death, these too were dignified with a special title, that of "Confessors". When the persecutions died down, and Christians experienced less tribulation from without, it would naturally be questioned whether this acceptable oblation of men's sufferings to Christ must altogether cease with the persecution which had occasioned them. The Circumcellion heretics claimed that they could win the crown of martyrdom by suicide; but the Church from the first disowned this interpretation; martyrdom might be prayed for, might be courted—it could not be self-inflicted. Did this necessarily apply to all the privations which the "Confessors" had had to undergo? Driven out by the threats of their heathen oppressors, Christians had "wandered about in sheep-skins, in goat-skins, being in want, afflicted, distressed . . . wandering in deserts, in mountains, and in dens and caves of the earth." Here they had experienced a liberation of the spirit and an intimacy with God which the crowded life of cities would not have afforded them. What if they should now adopt from choice the life which had hitherto been forced on them by necessity? This, surely, was the argument used by the Fathers of the Desert, from whom Christian asceticism is largely derived. Already, as far back as St. Paul, the ascetic principle had been conceded when the Church honoured virginity. It was only an extension of that principle, when men preferred solitude to company, silence to speech, poverty to worldly ambition.

What, then, is the motive of Catholic asceticism? It is as well to rid ourselves of false conceptions at once. There is, as I have already said, an Oriental notion that all material creatures, or certain material creatures, are in themselves evil; so (for example) some extreme temperance advocates would have us believe that fermented liquor was not meant for our use at all. That is an interesting theory; it has nothing to do with Catholicism. There is a stoical notion that discomfort is to be sought for its own sake, as a kind of human perfection; so men will bathe in the sea every day in all weathers and boast themselves to be "as hard as nails". That is a pardonable eccentricity, but it has nothing to do with Catholicism. It may even be true that men have sacrificed their careers, before now, to a blind instinct of self-humiliation. That may be a noble weakness; but it has nothing to do with Catholicism.

The whole effort of Catholic asceticism is to lay down some principle, or set of principles, by which we can relate our use of God's creatures to an end. The only true end of the Christian life is that of serving God and promoting his glory. How can our use of creatures—eating and drinking, sleeping and waking, enjoyment of sense, employment of time, etc.— be so regulated as to form a means towards that end? There are three possible attitudes, which do not exclude one another.

1. An attitude of thankfulness to God for his creatures. This is, of course, the duty of all Christians; and the most rigorous ascetic does not rid himself of the obligation; for, fast and watch as he may, he is still enjoying God's gifts. But all of us to some extent, many of us to a large extent, are in a position of choice; we can choose whether we shall accept or forgo some forms of enjoyment, e.g., going to the theatre. Some

further attitude, then, is demanded of one who wishes to live his own life, not merely to take things as they come.

2. An attitude of indifference, which is prepared to accept with equal gratitude all experiences, whether pleasing or contrary to nature, and leaves all choice between them to be dictated by obedience, by the need of others, by the inspiration of the moment, etc. This indifferent attitude is peculiarly suited to the needs of that order in the Church in whose ascetic teaching it figures most prominently—I mean the Society of Jesus. For they, as the freelances of the Church, must be prepared to turn their hands to anything—teaching, lecturing, preaching, parish work, administration—and their manner of life will necessarily be conditioned by circumstances. At the same time, it is an attitude that can only be acquired to the full by a high degree of interior mortification; it requires, plainly, a calculated watchfulness over your own thoughts for which some temperaments may well be unsuited.

3. An attitude of self-denial; i.e., of refusing God's gifts, or rather returning them gratefully into his hands, for a special purpose and under proper direction. The purpose in question is twofold. On the one side, we may be afraid that things which are good in themselves may absorb us to such an extent as to deny us leisure or inclination for constant attendance upon the thought of God; this, primarily, was the motive which determined Saint Francis in his love of poverty, and also in his distrust of secular learning. And on the other side, holding that suffering is our due as the punishment of our sins, we may be anxious to make reparation to God, by mortifying our senses, for the sinful use we have made of them—or even, at a higher level, for the sinful use which others have made and are making of them. This twofold notion of self-discipline and self-denial, of vigilance and of reparation, is clearly set forth in the prayers of the Church

during Lent and at the other penitential seasons. At such times, all those faithful Christians whose opportunities allow of it are called upon to exercise a public mortification in matters of diet. And, unless very exceptional circumstances excuse them from it, all Christians are called upon to make a mere gesture (as it were) of mortification by abstaining from flesh meat on Fridays.

It must be observed, that all the spiritual authors caution us against the danger of undertaking voluntary mortifications of our own without prudent direction from another. There are dangers, obviously, to health; dangers, also, of spiritual pride, and of unnecessary scruple. Most commonly, souls which are drawn towards these ascetic ideas find the opportunity for doing God's will by entering into associations, monasteries, or convents, which practise their own common rules of mortification and so avoid the danger of individual vagaries. The religious orders of the Church may be viewed under a thousand different aspects, and supply a thousand different needs; they teach, they tend the sick and the dying, they conduct retreats or missions, they serve parishes, they send missions to the heathen, and so on; but the primary purpose of every order is, explicitly, the sanctification of its own members; and there is not one of them but has certain ascetic rules, certain common principles of self-denial, which it cultivates by its seclusion from the world, and robs of self-consciousness by enjoining them under obedience.

Protestant devotion does not reject the notion of self-discipline, though in practice it lays little stress upon it, for fear of encouraging self-consciousness and scruple. But it does, except where it is openly based upon Catholic models among a section of Anglicans, repudiate the idea that reparation can be made for the sins of others, or even for one's own, by voluntary discomfort or suffering. What is done cannot be undone; to offer satisfaction for our sins is, as it were, to bribe Almighty God in the hope that he will overlook them. There is a certain fine sturdiness about this Protestant attitude, especially when it is based upon an absorbing conviction as to the all-sufficing Merits of Jesus Christ. But, for all that, it has probably been more powerful than any other influence in losing, for Protestantism, the hearts of human kind.

For, after all, the problem which bites most deeply into the mind, for which, above all, the world looks to religion for a solution, is the problem of suffering. Not all the possible triumphs of medicine will silence man's questionings in this matter. A. is the victim of a chronic and painful disease; his wife is in a mad-house; his son has been killed in a motor accident; his daughter is in a consumptive hospital. What is to be said to him? Will you tell him that this is a punishment inflicted on him for his sins? There is a lack of graciousness in the approach. Will you tell him that it is part of a common debt, owed unavoidably for the sinfulness of our race? He will still wonder why his back was chosen for the burden. Will you tell him that he has an excellent opportunity for practising resignation? It is true enough, but there is cold comfort here. The bowed head will not be raised to listen, until you can tell him that suffering, no less than action, is meritorious; that he who accepts suffering from the hand of God, no less than he who takes it upon himself, is helping, voluntarily, to make reparation for human sin, is filling up in his own flesh "that which is lacking in the sufferings of Christ". Faith is needed, God knows, to accept such consolation; but there is consolation in the idea that the human race has a solidarity, not only in its sins but in making satisfaction for its sins; and nowhere but in a Catholic or a would-be-Catholic theology will you find that Gospel preached.

I have spoken of Catholic asceticism; it will be expected, perhaps, that I should add something about what is ordinarily understood to be its complement, Catholic mysticism. I do not mean, however, to devote much space to the subject here, for several reasons. (1) That, whereas ascetic theology is often derided as superstitious, mystical theology is in our day treated with respect, on the principle of *omne ignotum pro magnifico*. It is well to remember that in the palmy days of Protestantism, in the eighteenth century particularly, England mocked as fanaticism what it now honours as spirituality. (2) That it is doubtful whether true mysticism (in the sense at least of conscious union with God) is the prerogative of Catholics alone; there seems to be no reason why a Protestant who is "in good faith" should not be a mystic, or even why a "good heathen" should not achieve a limited range of mystical experience in the light of natural theology. (3) That except to those for whom the supernatural is mere mythology, mysticism needs defence as little as it admits of explanation.

But I will say this, that there is a flavour of simplicity about Catholic mysticism which is not easily matched outside the Church. If you pick up some anthology of spiritual sayings, you will find that the non-Catholic mystics are for the most part philosophers like Plotinus, or poets like Henry Vaughan —they would have been philosophers, they would have been poets, even if they had not happened to find themselves as mystics. Whereas the Catholic mystics will be, as likely as not, elementary schoolboys like St. John of the Cross, or incorrigibly stupid novices like St. Margaret Mary. It is hard to believe that such people, if they had missed the career of sanctity, would have made their mark at all. Catholic piety, some think, breathes the atmosphere of the hothouse; strange, then, that there should be this wild-flower simplicity about our most cherished saints!

And this I will add, that mysticism is in its own element within the Catholic Church precisely because that Church has authority to try the spirit of her prophets and to pronounce upon their revelations. How often has it happened that the mystics of Protestantism have proved ineffective in the long run, have augmented dissension among Christians instead of advancing piety, just because no external check controlled them! The fantastic speculations of a Swedenborg or a Joanna Southcott, how they might have been restrained and redirected if only they had had guidance, instead of a following! With such souls, nothing but a Church which claims infallibility can exercise any effective control. Protestantism today is less feracious of visionaries. But, if more should arise, where is the religious organisation apart from ours that can contain their energies, and restrain their exuberance?

I have called this chapter "The Ambitions Catholics Honour"; not "The Ambitions Catholics Aim At"; for indeed, there are many Catholics who do not aim, consciously, at voluntary mortification, do not even accept the sufferings which come to them in a mortified spirit. But Catholics in general, however relaxed their own lives, do honour the careers in which this spirit of mortification is most visible. They will have their joke, often enough, at the expense of the religious orders, who have, after all, their human weaknesses. But you will not find a Catholic, unless he has quite lost the faith, making fun of the religious life, or suggesting that its ideals are misplaced. A Protestant, in proportion as his own spiritual pulses beat low, will tend to lose his standards of spirituality; a few heroes he has, no doubt, but religiosity in general becomes the object of his distrust. The lax Protestant suspects superior virtue; the lax Catholic admires a higher level of grace.

And if he admires that higher level of grace in his fellow-mortals, still more, while the life of faith beats in him, he honours the saints in heaven. No need for him to ask where heaven is, or whether, in the long run, that question has any meaning. He thinks of the saints always as alive, always as within hail. The great ones of the world live, indeed, in memory; public statues have set their features permanently on record, and the inspiration by which they lived may survive them for centuries. But their memory fades, when their own generation has died, into something abstract and impersonal; the man has become an idea. It is not so that the saints live; we conceive them—fondly, the sceptic will tell us—as personally intimate with us, as exercising a real influence, not as the source of a mental inspiration. St. Philip Neri and St. Anthony of Padua are alive to us, no less than the Little Flower.

And above them all—for who would concede that place of honour more anxiously than themselves?—stands the Virgin Mother of Christ, the sorrowful Mother of us all. Not less intimate because so high above us, not loved less personally because her munificence is so wide, she permeates the thought, the art, the poetry, the lives of Catholics with radiance as of a spring day, or of good news heard suddenly. Protestants have said that we deify her; that is not because we exaggerate the eminence of God's mother, but because they belittle the eminence of God. A creature miraculously preserved from sin by the indwelling power of the Holy Ghost—that is to them a Divine title, because that is all the claim their grudging theologies will concede, often enough, to our Lord himself. They refuse honour to the God-bearing Woman because their Christ is only a God-bearing Man. We, who know that God could (if he would) annihilate every existing creature without abating anything of his Blessedness or his Glory, are not afraid lest the honour done to his creature of perfect Womanhood should prejudice the honour due to him. Touchstone of Truth in the ages of controversy, Romance of the medieval world, she has not lost, with the rise of new devotions, any fragment of her ancient glory. Other lights may glow and dim as the centuries pass, she cannot suffer change; and when a Catholic ceases to honour her, he ceases to be a Catholic.

XVIII

Catholics and Those Outside

Nothing, probably, arouses more antagonism against the Church than her exclusiveness. The other Christianities, so far from insisting upon the old shibboleths which separate them from her and from one another, seem only to perpetuate their differences because it would not be possible, without these, to experience the thrill of fraternisation. They are creeping closer to one another for warmth, in a world unresponsive to their message; and the uncompromising attitude of the Catholic Church involves her in the odium which ever attaches to singularity. The inquirer into her doctrines may be attracted by all that is positive in what she teaches, and yet, as a child of his age, shrink from giving in his name to her allegiance because he shrinks from a negation. Can he "unchurch" the other denominations, satisfying as they do the spiritual needs of men wiser and better than himself? Nay, will he not have to go farther? Will he not have to exclude them, not merely from his communion on earth, but from his hopes of heaven? What else is meant by that grim tenet, "No salvation outside the Church"?

Let it be understood from the outset that there is one sense in which this principle is literally true, admitting of no

qualifications. Catholics believe that there is no other religious body in the world *through which* salvation can be pro-
cured. The fact of membership in any other religious body
than ours will not contribute to any man's welfare in eternity.
Let us suppose two brothers, both brought up and confirmed
as Anglicans. One, from a dislike of forms and ceremonies,
breaks away from his old associations and throws in his lot (let
us say) with the Society of Friends. Even here he does not
aspire to full membership; but he believes in our Lord, he
prays, he lives an upright life. His brother remains an Anglican, and wears his Anglicanism with a difference; he goes to
Confession and to Communion with exemplary regularity,
believes in the Real Presence, and puts his trust in the "undivided" Church. Now, from the Catholic point of view, there
is no more and no less hope of salvation in the one case than
in the other. Either is saved, if he is saved, under the same
title; namely that, in the sense to be explained lower down,
he is a Roman Catholic without knowing it.

In a word, we do not think of our Church as the best
religious body to belong to; we believe that those who do not
belong to it, provided that they believe in our Lord and desire
to do his will, may just as well belong to no religious body at
all. Even a schismatic Greek who is "in good faith", although
he receives valid Communion, and at the hour of death valid
absolution, is saved through Rome, not through Constan-
tinople. For it is normally necessary to salvation to hold the
Catholic Faith; and to believe in Catholic doctrines without
believing in the existence of that infallible authority which
guarantees them all is to hold, not the Catholic Faith, but a
series of speculative opinions. It is the first infidelity that
counts.

To that unique position the Catholic Church still lays claim;
save for a handful of sects, alone among the Christianities.

That is her continuous witness, from the times when the New Testament was written to our own. And yet it is true, I think, to say that Catholics in our own day are more ready to believe in the good faith of those outside the Church, and consequently to hope for their salvation, than Catholics were (say) in the Middle Ages. That is not an alteration of doctrine; it is rather a shifting of perspective. The question, whether and in what circumstances salvation is possible outside the visible unity of the Church, is a question which is felt to have more urgency in proportion as the imagination pictures the number of people affected. When the known world could be roughly divided into Catholics, Jews, and Mohammedans, it would hardly occur to a Catholic writer to consider whether the sporadic heresies of his day numbered among their adherents any who refused the authority of the Church through inculpable ignorance. Today, and especially in English-speaking countries, we are everywhere surrounded by Protestantism, and Protestantism nearly in the tenth generation; we are conscious that many of our neighbours live by high Christian ideals, and have an unaffected love of the truth. Naturally we are more ready to keep in mind that principle of Catholic theology which deals with those who hold religious errors "in good faith".

Pius IX has enunciated the principle for us very clearly: "Those who are hampered by invincible ignorance about our Holy Religion, and, keeping the natural law, with its commands that are written by God in every human heart, and being ready to obey him, live honourably and uprightly, can, with the power of Divine light and grace helping them, attain eternal life. For God, who clearly sees, searches out, and knows the minds, hearts, thoughts, and dispositions of all, in his great goodness and mercy does not by any means suffer a man to be punished with eternal torments, who is not guilty of voluntary fault." It may be added that invincible ignorance is defined as "that which has not been capable of being overcome or removed by reasonable care; whether because no thought or doubt concerning such matters ever entered the mind; or because, even if such a thought had come into the mind, this ignorance could not have been overcome or removed by the use of reasonable and common care, nor could a knowledge of the truth have been obtained."

It was at one time held by certain theologians, chiefly under St. Augustine's influence, that "original sin" carried with it, through the solidarity of the human race, a taint of personal guilt. It would follow from this that an infant, dying unbaptised, must be condemned to some form of positive suffering in a future world. From this consequence St. Augustine did not shrink; it is clear, however, that this was not the unanimous opinion of the early Church, since Gregory of Nazianzum can be quoted in the opposite sense. From the time of the schoolmen onwards, a more reasonable view has prevailed; viz., that original sin is no source of personal guilt, and the unbaptised infant is therefore free from all that "pain of sense" by which personal guilt is punished. The Jansenist influence endeavoured, but ineffectually, to procure a condemnation of this milder view; and it is obvious that the Catechism of the Council of Trent does not attempt a decision of the question when it says that unbaptised infants remain *in statu miseriæ*, a phrase which is perfectly well understood as merely contrasting the natural with the supernatural life.[1] The opinion is now universal amongst Catholics that, although these infants are excluded from that supernatural vision of God to which our nature does not entitle us, they

---

[1] *Miseria* is the scholastic opposite of *felicitas* (*Summa* II/2, 30, 1.), and the felicity here in question is the supernatural felicity which consists in the vision of God.

nevertheless enjoy some kind of natural happiness; and the opinion which stigmatised this doctrine of Limbo as "a Pelagian fable" was condemned by Pius VI as false, rash, and injurious to Catholic teaching. On what principle it is that certain souls are chosen to enjoy (through baptism) a higher state of felicity, without ever becoming capable of a moral choice, he knows who created them, and who can tell what they would have made of their lives had life been granted to them.

But, once a man has attained the age of reason, he is bound (Catholic theology teaches) for one of two ultimate destinies, fixed and eternal—hell or heaven; and this is true even of those myriads of souls which have never had the opportunity, or never had full opportunity, to hear the Christian message preached; true of those many souls which have never inherited any intelligent tradition of Theism. All of these, in proportion as invincible ignorance debarred them from the truth, will be judged according to the lights they had. It is not difficult to see that such ignorance may extend to the principles of natural morality, or rather to their application. Thus, we hold that suicide is a contravention of the natural law written in men's hearts. But, where an Indian widow commits suicide in accordance with an immemorial fashion, or where an Otho prefers his own death to the ruin of his country, is it not natural to assume that, although their consciences were misinformed, they acted according to the highest lights they had? Theologians may disagree as to the manner in which such unbaptised souls achieve "the baptism of desire"; whether the fact that they would have sought baptism if they had known about it is sufficient to justify them, or whether some special revelation must be postulated to account for their salvation. But the fact remains clear—nobody goes to hell except through his own fault; and those who are the beneficiaries of this principle *must* therefore attain heaven, by whatever means and upon whatever title.

These considerations clearly do not apply to those who, having once obtained the grace of faith through baptism, and arrived at an intelligent appreciation of Christian tenets, abandon their belief in favour of agnosticism or of some rival religion. That failure of the mental powers can be held to excuse such a change of sentiments is evident from the controversy which arose over the later speculations of Mivart, and the ecclesiastical sanction which ultimately granted him Christian burial. It may well be that some of those whom we regard as formal apostates were not responsible for their apparently sane decisions. It may well be that others never really "left" the faith, because in fact, through defect of education, the faith had never been in them. It is difficult not to believe that the absence of all priestly ministrations sometimes causes, especially among the uneducated, inculpable lapses from Christian unity. But such charitable speculations will not always be in place; and there are careers upon which no optimistic epitaph can be pronounced, except the hope that some change of heart, outwardly unattested, may have saved the unhappy soul from the guilt of final impenitence.

But, whereas it is normal to assume that one who takes the initiative in heresy will be held responsible for his disloyalty to Catholic doctrine, it would be unreasonable to argue that one born and bred in heresy, who does not "see his way" to accepting the Catholic Faith, lies under the same condemnation. All the traditions of his thought, all the prejudices of his race and caste, all the influence of his friends and teachers, has been thrown into the opposite scale; the *vis inertiæ* tells not for but against his chances of being a Catholic. Meanwhile, he has probably received valid baptism; the habit of faith, then, has been implanted in him, and those circumstances of environment and education which have made him a heretic are not imputable to him as a fault; he has not wilfully sinned against it. So long, therefore, as he does not come in contact with the Catholic system at all, or does not come across it in such a way as to be effectively challenged by its claims, he has not refused grace. So long as he takes all reasonable pains to study those claims in a fairminded spirit, and still, through some defect of outlook, of temperament, of intellectual apparatus, finds himself drawn no nearer to the truth, he has not refused grace. His ignorance is, so far as we can tell, of the invincible kind; he remains what he is "in good faith". If he falls into grave sin he has, of course, no access to sacramental absolution; but it is still possible for him to make that perfect act of contrition which claims forgiveness. We have no fears for such heretics as this.

But, we must repeat, it is not through adhesion to any other religious body that such a man can qualify for membership in our Church, as by a kind of *ad eundem* degree. Rather, he is a lonely satellite of the Church's system that has lost its true orbit. And it should be added that this plea of "good faith" is one which may be urged on behalf of the Protestant, but it is not one which he can urge in his own behalf. A man can say, "You are in good faith", "He is in good faith", but not "I am in good faith"—that is to beg the question. The attitude of mind—painfully common—which says, "I am not qualified to go into all these complicated credentials of the Catholic Church", is an attitude of intellectual indolence masquerading as intellectual humility. The man who "thinks there may be something in it", yet makes no effort to find out how much, is actuated not by invincible but by supine ignorance. The man who (worse still) excuses himself from examining our credentials *for fear lest he should find them to be true*; who tells you that he is too busy to consider the Catholic claim, or too modest, or too unadventurous, when at the back of his mind he is shrinking from the injury to his prospects, the troubles with his family which submission to the Church would involve—such a man is actuated not by invincible but by affected ignorance. And, I am sorry to say it, I believe there is much supine ignorance, much affected ignorance, among our fellow-countrymen. Let them not deceive themselves; they will have to find another title to heaven if they are to attain heaven at all.

I must add a word here, lest I should be accused of "burking" the subject, about the attitude which the Church holds on the subject of coercion in spiritual matters. There is no space here to reason with those whose fancies are obsessed with the horrors of the Inquisition to such an extent that they cannot speak calmly of it. But those who are more skilled in analysing their own antipathies may be invited to consider the following distinctions. The employment of torture by the Inquisition was in accordance with the judicial practice of the time, as Protestant England can witness. It is utterly out of accord with the spirit of our own age, and a Catholic authority would be no more likely to inflict it now than a Protestant authority. The death-penalty, which a hundred and fifty years ago was still inflicted for such crimes as horse-stealing, has similarly passed out of vogue except in dealing with brutalised characters; and I see no reason to think that it would ever be re-enacted for religious offences, however much Catholicism should gain ground in the counsels of nations. So far as "atrocities" are concerned, Catholics may well be thankful that we have got rid of them, though we shall beg leave to insist that Catholic tribunals had no monopoly of such proceedings.

But a more intimate doubt assails the liberal temperament. Is it just, since thought is free, to penalise *in any way* differences of speculative outlook? Ought not every Church, however powerful, to act as a body corporate within the State, exercising no form of coercion except that of exclusion from its own spiritual privileges? It is very plain that this has not been the Catholic theory in times past. There has been, in Catholic nations, a definite alliance between the secular and the spiritual power. So, to be sure, has there been among Protestant nations. But may it be understood that in our enlightened age Catholics would repudiate the notion of any such alliance in future?

It must be freely admitted that this is not so. You cannot bind over the Catholic Church, as the price of your adhesion to her doctrines, to waive all right of invoking the secular arm in defence of her own principles. The circumstances in which such a possibility could be realised are indeed sufficiently remote. You have to assume, for practical purposes, a country with a very strong Catholic majority, the overwhelming body of the nation. Probably (though not certainly) you would have to assume that the non-Catholic minority are innovators, newly in revolt against the Catholic system, with no ancestral traditions, no vested interests to be respected. Given such circumstances, is it certain that the Catholic government of the nation would have no right to insist on the Catholic religion being taught in all schools open to the general public, and even to deport or imprison those who unsettled the minds of its subjects with new doctrines?

It is certain that the Church would claim that right for the Catholic Government, even if considerations of prudence forbade its exercise in fact. The Catholic Church will not be one amongst the philosophies. Her children believe, not that her doctrines may be true, but that they are true, and consequently part of the normal make-up of a man's mind; not even a parent can legitimately refuse such education to his child. They recognise, however, that such truths (unlike the mathematical axioms) can be argued against; that simple minds can easily be seduced by the sophistries of plausible error; they recognise, further, that the divorce between speculative belief and practical conduct is a divorce in thought, not in fact; that the unchecked developments of false theories result in ethical aberrations—Anabaptism yesterday, Bolshevism to-day—which are a menace even to the social order.

Such considerations would reasonably be invoked if a body of Catholic patriots, entrusted with the government of a Catholic State, should deny to the innovator the right of spreading his doctrines publicly, and so endangering the domination of Catholic principles among their fellow-countrymen.

It is frequently argued, that if Catholics have at the back of their system such notions of "toleration", it is unreasonable in them to complain when a modern State restricts, in its turn, the political or educational liberty which they themselves wish to enjoy. What is sauce for the goose is sauce, surely, for the gander. The contention is ill-conceived. For, when we demand liberty in the modern State, we are appealing to its own principles, not to ours. The theory of the modern State is that all religions should be equally tolerated, as long as they do not disturb the peace or otherwise infringe the secular laws of the country; we only claim to share that right amongst the rest. The philosophic basis on which the modern State rests its theory is that Truth is great and will prevail; a false system of religion will condemn itself in the end by its own unreason-ableness, without external interference. Does it fear, then, our religion, more than others? And if so, on what grounds, unless it be on the somewhat paradoxical ground that our religion is true? If the Church is persecuted by men with strong religious convictions, she offers the dumb protest of martyrdom. It is when she is persecuted by men who loudly proclaim they have none, that she ventures to tax them with inconsistency.

In a word, the unity of the Church has hard edges. Of this our Protestant ancestors did not complain; they had their hard edges too. Our generation, suckled on the milk of nineteenth-century liberalism, still hankers after cloudy formulas and indefinite compromise. But is this mood of vagueness permanent? In an era which has produced Bolshevism and Fascism, it seems a pardonable doubt.

XIX

Catholicism and the Future

If the Church is criticised in religious circles for her indifference to the Reunion movement, she disappoints the more
secular-minded once more by an attitude of negation.
Wrapped up in her own ambitions for recovering the lost
allegiance of humanity, she appears to view all schemes for
the social betterment of mankind at best with tolerance, and
commonly with suspicion. We have inherited from the Victorian Age the dogma of human progress. No age can live
without an inspiration; when religious inspiration disappears,
as it has very largely disappeared from the modern world,
man's capacity for self-sacrificing devotion to a Cause must
find its outlet in other channels. Here and there, if political
grievances or other accidents of history have sharpened the
edge of nationality, a people can find its inspiration in purely
patriotic movements. Elsewhere, no enthusiasm is left to us
except an enthusiasm for humanity at large; and this is not
easily kindled by a contemplation of the human species as it
now is. Those restless spirits, therefore, which cannot be
happy unless they are working for an ideal, must pin their
faith to a regenerate world of tomorrow. When mechanical
invention has made life still easier for us, and medicine has

made it still more comfortable for us; when selective breeding has eliminated from our ranks those who are C3 men[1] in the battle of life; when education has made us more fit to occupy our leisure upon worthy objects, more responsive to the thrill of noble ideals; when a redistribution of wealth at home, and a new sense of world-solidarity, have put an end to our antagonisms—then we shall have produced a race worth fighting for and worth working for; then we shall have established, with no help from super-nature, a kingdom of heaven on earth.

It is a matter of observation that Catholics do not commonly echo this sonorous phraseology of our time. Does that mean that the Catholic system is itself incompatible with such hopes of improvement, or merely that Catholics are too much preoccupied with other considerations to spare any time for these? It would be easy to construct a mere debating reply to the criticism; it might be pointed out that in countries like ours, where Catholics are a minority of the population, their first concern, the first demand on their time and attention, is to consolidate the position of their own Church. Or, again, that the hostile attitude shown by the "progressive" parties in several Continental countries has forced the Church into a distrust of all such developments. Or (what is nearer the truth) it might be said that the Church is primarily concerned with the individual soul as a single unit; and that the most striking and most characteristic of the activities set on foot by her children are out of harmony with the spirit of the time precisely because they take the individual soul, here and now, as their point of departure, instead of being concerned with the fortunes of a class, or of mankind in general. How much of Catholic charity is wasted (from the world's point of view)

---

[1] The lowest category in the medical examination for service in the armed forces is C; thus C3 denotes a weakling.

upon the lepers, the incurable, the dying, the dying races, too, and the sinful souls that will never "make good"!

But there is, if we will but have the patience to analyse the situation and the honesty to admit it, a real difference of view in this whole matter between the Church and the moderns. The moderns believe, the Church does not believe, in the perfectibility of the human character on a large scale; that is the long and short of it.

To the moderns, the notion of a continual improvement in the human race is both an axiom of thought and a dogma of faith. An axiom of thought, for if you question it they suspect you of joking. A dogma of faith, for it is what they live by; the glaring tragedy of life would be too much for them, if they had no outlook beyond the present, and its indefinite continuance. It is a moral which they deduce, with some hesitations of method, from the developments of history. It is a corollary which they infer, with no very good title, from the scientific hypothesis of Evolution. Economic history, even, is subpœnaed to prove the case; Capitalism itself is treated as a stage in the development towards higher things. The *expression* of such confidence in the future is out of date, Victorian; but the confidence itself is none the less deep in men's hearts, because unuttered.

I sometimes fancy that even if the Catholic Church had no doctrine bearing on the point, she would still smile, in the wisdom she has garnered from experience, at the pathetic optimism of our modern visionaries. Who has not known some old, perfectly mellowed schoolmaster, trained by long experience to adopt a double attitude towards youth—infinite patience with the individual, and a profound distrust of the type? So many short-lived generations have passed through his hands, and he has watched them make the same mistakes, cultivate the same poses, suffer from the same conviction of their own originality; no, the type does not alter, it is for him to do the best he can with the material that is given him. And the Catholic Church, since the day when she was sent to teach all nations, is much in the schoolmaster's position; there is no trend of philosophy, no movement in politics, no nation, even, in Europe, which does not seem young to her. And should she not be tempted to doubt, even on experimental grounds, the perfectibility of the human character? She has seen that magnificent creature of man, the Roman Empire, grow to its full strength and then crumble into a dust-heap of nationalities; she has watched chieftaincy grow into kingship, and kingship fade into constitutional monarchy; she has witnessed the epic tragedy of the Crusades; she has seen the rise and the decadence of Bible Protestantism, and Ridley's candle guttering in its socket; she has seen the French Revolution spring up, and blossom into a tyranny; slavery die, and Industrialism replace it; aristocracy fail, and plutocracy rise on its ruins; she has stood by while three great empires vanished in two years, while men beat their swords into ploughshares, and then smelted their ploughshares into high explosives; commercial world-hegemony has passed from Spain to France, from France to England, from England to the United States; and, to her longer memory, every experiment seems by the fashion of a time, every rebirth of ours abortive. We do not repeat the same mistakes precisely; here and there the failure of our ancestors has blazed the trail for us. But is the world really reaching a Promised Land? Or is it wandering, like Israel, forty years in the wilderness?

The hesitation, I say, might be pardoned in her, even if no revealed doctrine lent credence to it. But theology tells her that Man is a fallen creature; and, were she tempted to be a thousand times more optimistic over his future, she would still despair of his perfectibility on this side of the grave. Here and there, she tells us, a soul full of heroic sanctity will spring up in our midst, like a sport of Nature; now and again the impetus of some great movement will stampede a whole multitude of souls into unwonted generosity of purpose; but in the long run Adam's taint will be for ever breaking out in his posterity, new efforts will be needed to reclaim humanity, new ideals to inspire it. It is this settled mood of pessimism, almost of cynicism, in her that scandalises the ardent temperament of our world-reformers. She will not believe, with them, that our race can ever be endowed, through human means, with indefectible virtue. She lets us build our sand-castles, but depresses us with the reminder that the tide will carry them away.

The Church's attitude, then, is dogmatic, but here it is no more dogmatic than the attitude of her opponents. Where, after all, can we find any proof that the human type is perfecting, any notion, even, whither the history of its process is developing? There is a modern tendency—Mr. Wells, in his "Outline of History", is its exponent—to dwarf the whole pedigree of our civilisation, to shorten the whole perspective of events, by pointing us back to the long ages which elapsed before history itself began—those successive "periods" which the geologists find it necessary to postulate in co-ordinating their hitherto achieved results. No wonder, these authors suggest, that you cannot find any real development in the human type between Babylon yesterday and Washington to-day—that is because you have chosen too short a section of the process. To recognise the past from which we came, and forecast the future which lies before us, you must contrast the humanity of today, not with that of the cuneiform inscriptions, but with that which left us our earliest cave-drawings. Can we pretend that the human species has not advanced in culture since it lived the grimy, brutish existence of Halbert and Hob?

But the process is *obscurum per obscurius*. We know something about the minds of the men who have left us organised writing; we know nothing of the men who have left us, boy-like, a picture or two on the walls—not even whether it was men or boys that drew them. They could draw men and women about as well as I can; animals very much better than I can; that is a boy's trick. But I do not know whether the human figures were portraits of friends or caricatures of enemies or images of gods. I do not know whether the bones of their friends were painted red out of some funeral piety, or whether the bones of their enemies were painted red in savage triumph. You cannot accept the bushman as a representative of primitive culture until you can be certain that he has not degenerated like the Aztecs. In short, if you want to base your dogma of human progress upon facts, they must be the facts which are yielded by historical, not by merely archæological records.

Still less will you derive any support from going back behind the human species altogether, and attempting to link up the progress of mankind with the theory of biological evolution. Biology knows of nothing except "survival values"; the qualities which it holds up for our admiration are qualities which enable the species to avoid destruction, whether by means of superior attack or of superior defence. But the moral values which mankind has agreed to revere are not those which tend to preserve the species. The charity which provides for the sick in hospitals, for the lunatics in asylums, is cumbering the earth with useless weeds, with unproductive consumers; and that at a time when (the wise-acres tell us) our common food-supply will barely suffice our growing needs for another century. Evolution clamours that these inferior specimens of the race should be eliminated; morality revolts from the doctrine. It is not because of Nature, but in spite of Nature, that philanthropy has come to embarrass us.

What, then, are the facts which emerge from an unbiased study of history about the progress of Man? It is certain that, by a merely mechanical law, the comfort of his surroundings increases; the useful arts, once discovered, are not suffered to die out; we can avoid pain, we can annihilate distance, we can produce the means of gratification more readily than our ancestors could. Probably we are becoming, in a corresponding measure, softer than they; habituation to comforts has reduced, though within curiously defined limits, the hardiness of our physique. No doubt, again, but Man has become a more complicated creature in a thousand ways; his aesthetic appreciations are subtler, his intellect more active, his outlook more individualised; even his appreciation of moral issues more acute. But does Man obey, with more and more facility as the centuries roll by, those interior monitions of conscience which claim to wield an influence over his behaviour?

It is certainly true that institutions have disappeared from the greater part of the world, it would seem permanently, whose disappearance every Christian must welcome. (Whether the non-Christian welcomes it equally, depends upon his point of view.) Formal slavery has disappeared, and physical torture used for judicial purposes, and the exposure of children, and the amphitheatre, and the duel, and child labour, and the grosser forms of purposeless cruelty towards animals. But these are not vices personal to the individual; they are vicious systems, against which the conscience of individuals long protested, before the community took any steps. The progressive enlightenment of the public conscience is fortunately a fact; though it is not certain what guarantee we have against retrogression. But the fact that the public obeys its own conscience is due, if we will be honest with ourselves, very largely to the policeman. The really salient fact about the modern age, from the Wars of the Roses onwards, is the growing effectiveness of centralised government, ultimately traceable to the influence of explosives. Not only have we better laws, but our laws are better kept. Where morality involves justice towards your neighbour, there is less temptation to do wrong now than formerly; indeed, there is every temptation to do right. But does all this mean that, given the free opportunity, the average man today resists his temptations, such as they are, better than he did in the Dark Ages?

There is, as far as I am aware, no theological reason why this should not be so; why there should not, I mean, be a certain moral improvement, as time goes on, in the general level of mankind; theology only assures us that we cannot "breed out" altogether that concupiscence which the Fall has left behind it. But as a matter of fact there seems to be little ground for assuming that any such improvement has taken place. It is easy to say, for example, that drunkenness is less common now than it used to be. But does that really mean that our generation is more self-disciplined than its predecessors? When you reflect on the various influences that have checked drunkenness—the deterrent efforts of the Law, the decline in robustness of physique, the artificial inflation of prices, the change of manners which operates on our instincts of social cowardice, and so on—it is hard to be impressed by the statistics. Circumstances restrict our opportunities for self-indulgence, and a modern squeamishness of taste moderates its grosser forms; but this is not a change of heart.

Let it be said at once that no Christian and no Catholic can fail to rejoice when he finds the temptations to wrong-doing diminished by legal or social coercion, so long as Man's common liberties are respected. No body of men in the country has, I suppose, more cogent reason to deplore the bad conditions under which poor families live, than the Catholic clergy. Grinding poverty is a well-known enemy not only to morals but to faith itself. But always our primary preoccupation is to help men make the best of the conditions in which they find themselves; whereas the primary preoccupation of the modern reformer is to better the conditions and to hope for a new race of men. Our work is to colonise heaven, theirs to breed for Utopia. And that disparity of inspiration leads, again and again, to a contrast of method. The revolutionary reformer wishes to achieve Utopia by methods which offend against our sense of justice. The bureaucratic reformer wishes to achieve Utopia by methods which offend against our sense of liberty. Neither side finds in us an ally who can be trusted to go all lengths; either side, therefore, distrusts our alliance, and at best tolerates it as a necessary embarrassment.

It seems probable enough that the Armageddon of the future lies between Catholicism and some form of humanitarianism—I mean the attempt (in some form) to produce a perfect humanity through the external pressure of breeding, education, and legal coercion. Some writers have, perhaps, made this forecast with undue confidence; history has not yet forgotten how to cheat the prophets. But our modern symptoms do, it must be admitted, point that way. More and more, it appears, men's loyalties fluctuate between the extremes of supernaturalism and materialism; the less definite Christianities are moulds in which they settle, but do not harden. If these attract, they attract precisely where they are content to approximate to either extreme, by wearing with a difference the world's colours or ours.

It is not safe to prophesy the disappearance of any religious body; it is their way to linger on, skeleton armies, long after their effectiveness has spent itself. But the *tendency* of modern religion is away from moderate counsels; it is admitted even by many who deplore it. Already we Catholics are embarrassed by unwelcome admirers—on the Continent, by authoritarians who reject the supernatural, in England, by sacramentalists who reject authority. It will not be wonderful if the second generation from ours finds clearer issues presented to it in the world's debate.

Meanwhile, the ethos of Catholics is not futuristic; they live, not on dreams, but on convictions. They witness without surprise the depopulation of religion around them; we have been told beforehand that the days will come when charity shall wax cold. Yet they do not (like some Protestant enthusiasts) look round them eagerly for the signs of an approaching world-dissolution; they have heard the cry of "Wolf!" too often. They devote themselves, rather, to the business of their own souls, and to influencing, in whatever modest way may be practicable, the lives of those around them, secure of inviolable principles and of a hope which cannot fade. He that believeth, let him not make haste—it is commonly, among Catholics themselves, where faith is weakest that clamour is loudest, for a policy and a world-attitude. "But you, beloved, building yourselves upon your most holy faith, praying in the Holy Ghost, keep yourselves in the love of God, waiting for the mercy of our Lord Jesus Christ unto life everlasting."